THE Sodfather

An Extraordinary Journey in the Shadows of Sports' Greatest Fields

While every precaution has been taken in the preparation of this book, the publisher assumes no responsibility for errors or omissions, or for damages resulting from the use of the information contained herein. In recounting the events for this book, some details have been compressed, altered, and omitted to better fit the narrative. Some of the dialogue has been changed and/or abbreviated.

THE SODFATHER
AN EXTRAORDINARY JOURNEY
IN THE SHADOWS OF SPORTS' GREATEST FIELDS

First edition. May 1, 2024.

Published by Big Kat Kreative LLC, 2024.
Printed in the United States of America.

Cover designed by Michael Mazewski of Big Kat Kreative
Cover photo taken by Donna Toma

ISBN: 978-1-962796-04-0

Written by George Toma and Craig Handel.

THE Sodfather

An Extraordinary Journey in the Shadows of Sports' Greatest Fields

GEORGE TOMA
WITH CRAIG HANDEL

Dedicated to all groundskeepers.
This fraternity of hard-working pros provides
safe playing fields, which is the cheapest insurance
in the world for athletes of all ages – from
preschoolers to professionals.

Dedicated to all family members.
They're the ones who sacrificed, they're the ones who
saw my faults and quirks and yet they still love me.

Contents

Foreword 1
Introduction 7

1: Coal Miner's Son 13
2: Eight-Decade Career Begins 18
3: Kansas City Here I Come 25
4: Scramble Drill 37
5: Super Endorsements 50
6: Superball, Super Bowl 58
7: Carpet vs. Sod 66
8: Super Bowl Evolves 76
9: Nicknames, Friends, Honors 89
10: Tricks Of The Trade 104
11: The Flood, The Field, The Catch ... 117
12: Taming Mother Nature 125
13: Have Rake, Will Travel 131
14: Chip Off The Old Block 144
15: Shark Gets Bitten 154
16: Sodgate 158
17: Calling George Toma 167
18: Hollow Words 173
19: Roger And Out 184
20: Frustration Mounts 188
21: Prelude To A Disaster 196
22: Super Streak Ends 207
23: Toma Tales 212
24: Are The Owners Listening 222
25: Leaving Legacies 228

Acknowledgments 239
Final Thoughts 257
Toma Timeline 263
About The Authors 275

Foreword

George Toma's career spanned parts of nine decades, which led to many colorful interactions within the industry. That longevity is why the foreword needed three colleagues to share their unique encounters with him to properly introduce this trailblazer and legendary groundskeeper.

Bill Beck, Major League Baseball Executive

George is one of the most remarkable individuals I have known during my 48-year baseball career. I first met the man on July 4, 1968, at Municipal Stadium in Kansas City, and it immediately started with fireworks.

Why do I remember the date?

The soccer game that night was the Santos Club of Brazil vs. the Kansas City Spurs of the old North American Soccer League, and I was thrilled to broadcast the event.

The match featured the highest-paid athlete in the world at the time, Pele, and all he did was score a goal and register an assist in the 4-1 Santos win.

I entered the old ballpark through the center-field gate and carried broadcast equipment. As I started to cut across the green field, I heard a voice shout out, "Get off the field!" It startled me, as I was headed to the press box. I stated the equipment was heavy, but that made no impression. Again, "Get off the field!" rang out. I retreated and walked along the warning track. You guessed correctly; that was George protecting his turf.

That was my introduction to George Toma, and to this day, I have never forgotten how beautiful the field looked that evening. It was an unusual start to a friendship that has spanned many decades. As I later learned, George had a habit of yelling at people to stay off the grass, even with well-known and successful people.

George and I reconnected in 1975 when we were both employed by the Kansas City Royals. He was great at working with real-grass fields. Unfortunately, starting in 1973 when Royals Stadium (now Kauffman Stadium) opened, the playing surface was artificial turf. I know he put every ounce of energy into keeping the surface as pristine as possible. His crew and he hated sunflower seeds, bubble gum and tobacco juice on or in the turf. The artificial field was as good as it could possibly be. He worked for the Royals for more than 30 years and also assisted ownership, staff members and friends with their lawns. Both the Royals and Kansas City Chiefs went back to real grass turf in the mid-'90s.

A handful of people went to the first 57 Super Bowls, with George being one of those individuals.

I was on the field with George along with 1,000 people for Super Bowl XXXIII in Miami Gardens, Fla., in 1999. Friday before the Sunday game was dress rehearsal for the national anthem and halftime show. This happens at every Super Bowl and can't be avoided. George kept looking at the grass and was ready to make any repairs necessary when the session was over.

The pride in his work was always unmatched.

This book and all its chapters are entertaining and a great and easy read. You will enjoy the stories and marvel at the people with whom George dealt. His reach was far beyond Major League Baseball and the National Football League. Enjoy this Horatio Alger story about a man who excelled after humble beginnings.

Mike Albino, Turf Manager, Consultant
Let me start off by making one thing perfectly clear: George Toma is a no-nonsense type of guy with a huge heart.

George's work ethic is guided by his "and then some" attitude, which has taken him from poverty to international recognition. His specialty is working; he knows how to make things happen. I have seen his willingness to work with you as a great boss or next to you on his hands and knees getting the job done.

He is dedicated to his job and is willing to share his knowledge and teach anyone wanting to learn. He will not waste his time teaching if you are a slacker.

He is showing you because that is the way things are done. He is sharing a lifetime of experience to help make you better at your job.

George does not take any action to be hurtful. I have seen him rip into someone, then 20 minutes later, he will bring that person a cup of coffee and have a chat with them. Why? First, they had it coming, and second, he is a dedicated teacher.

He knows how to deal with people. George can talk to anyone and do it at his or her level. He is a good listener, and, above all, he is a great storyteller. His stories involve the various people he has met, such as Roger Maris and Mickey Mantle.

He also has worked with the guys in the Negro Leagues Baseball Museum and the groundskeepers. They still keep in touch with him to let him know how much they appreciate him. Mr. Toma is a walking legend and can hold an audience's attention for hours.

I got to know George's son Chip and used to go to Fort Myers, Fla., with him and George when they were working at the Minnesota Twins' spring training complex. Chip really did a good job when he was running things; he knew what he was doing. When you talked to Chip, it was like talking to George. Chip is a really good guy, and I'd even say he is a chip off the old block.

You would have to walk a long way to find a person as

principled and honorable as George Toma.

That's why I'm honored to call him a friend!

Jim Steeg, Sports Management, Media Consulting

My first experience with George Toma was on Jan. 21, 1979, at Super Bowl XIII in Miami. I had started with the National Football League on Jan. 3 and was assigned to observe how things operated at the game.

I was told to assist on the field operations for that game. The halftime show that year was a salute to the Caribbean that involved a 120-yard tarp designed to look like the Caribbean that covered from goal post to goal post. Then there was a native band representing each island, and a boat would travel from island to island, then each band would play. The rehearsals went smoothly. But on game day, at the end of the first half, the tarp was brought out. It was to be rolled down the middle of the field, then to each sideline.

There was an issue. The volunteers brought the tarp too far to the west end zone beyond the goal post. It was impossible to move back. The northwest corner of the tarp was stuck by the goal post.

It was at that moment when I heard someone bellow, "Anyone have a knife?"

Simultaneously about 10 knives were thrown from the stands onto the field.

Who was the person who yelled for the knives? George Toma.

I will never forget that moment as the knives came raining down on the field. The tarp was cut, and as they say, "The show went on."

Over the next 26 years, I would come to appreciate George as the ultimate professional and problem solver. He and I would work together throughout the United States and in multiple venues overseas. He became the person who would always execute a plan flawlessly.

Each year there were unique challenges for the game and practice fields, but George always found a way to overcome them. Among those obstacles were:

- Building practice fields out of grass areas at the University of North Florida for Super Bowl XXXIX in 2005 and also creating one out of an undeveloped area at the University of South Florida at Super Bowl XXXV in 2001.
- Measuring the Metrodome field at Super Bowl XXVI in 1992 and discovering that it was only 119 yards long.
- There was an infestation of birds in San Diego for Super Bowl XXII in 1988, and he had to figure a way to keep them from eating the seed on the field.
- He completely built two fields at Scottsdale Community College for Super Bowl XXX in 1996. Then we discovered that the Fiesta Bowl teams used the fields and the University of Nebraska destroyed them. So, George had to redo the fields in 20 days.
- In Minnesota, he decided to replace the base outlines on the field two hours before kickoff.

Each halftime show was a challenge, as the production people always wanted more time on the field to rehearse than they were allotted. George babysat each one and solved many problems. One I remember well was at Super Bowl XXII in 1988 when the producer, Radio City, went against our advice and designed a stage built on casters. Of course, when the rehearsal started, the casters broke. The stage had to be removed by forklift, and our jack-of-all-trades, Noel Lesley, replaced the casters with proper wheels.

When I was assigned to plan American Bowls in Berlin and Barcelona, I insisted that George be part of the team. The fields were perfect, and in the case of Barcelona, he built a perfect practice field on literally a dirt patch. He even shipped baseball bats with his tools. We would play baseball games on the Maifeld in Berlin and the Olympic baseball field in Barcelona, except he forgot the bats in 1994. Ever tried to find a baseball bat in Spain?

George would always go along with my ideas and make them work. I wanted to diversify the crew and suggested

Heather Nabozny of the Tigers. She joined the crew. I mentioned a new type of turf designed by professional golfer Greg Norman. He went along, and even though there were issues, he made it work.

Because George was working for the Royals, he always indulged me with my desire to play baseball. One year, the NFL annual meeting was in Orlando, Fla., and the Royals were training a half-hour away in Baseball City. I would go over each night and hit in the batting cage, which he supervised. On the Friday after the meeting, I went over to hit balls all day. The Royals were in Tampa that day, so I got free rein over the batting cages.

After a couple of hours, I came into the locker room to get some work on blisters that had developed from swinging the bat endlessly. As I was getting fixed, a guy came up to me and asked what I was doing. He admired me working through the pain and volunteered to give me some instruction because I was a friend of George's. That guy was Royals Hall of Famer George Brett.

One of my greatest honors was when George received the Ralph Hay Pioneer Award from the Pro Football Hall of Fame in 2001. He wanted me to give the introduction speech. It was a moment I will forever remember.

George Toma is truly a living legend. He has seen the National Football League grow since 1966 and always brought innovation to ensuring that the athletes would have the best playing surface possible. He had the skill to make all those who worked with and for him perform at their best and accomplish better than they thought they could.

I am so fortunate to have been able to work by his side and to call him a dear friend.

Introduction

For more than 80 years, I had the privilege of doing something I've always enjoyed immensely – working on athletic fields all over the world.

After losing my dad at age 11, I was blessed to have a number of people – family members, big-brother types, father figures and others I call angels – who taught me the value of working hard while helping me find my way through life.

Among them was Emil Bossard, the greatest groundskeeper ever. Using his creativity and ingenuity, he taught me how to use my mind as well as my body to manipulate, manicure and beautify earth and grass. At my core, I'm a dirt man. I also have worked with incredibly talented and dedicated people to make some of the greatest sports venues in the world safer and aesthetically pleasing.

My journey started in Wilkes-Barre, Pa., as an assistant groundskeeper, and it has taken me to such places as Charleston, W.Va.; Los Angeles; New Orleans; Honolulu; Berlin; Kibbutz Gezer, Israel; and every corner of Florida.

But my home base is in Kansas City, where I have lived there for more than 65 years. It's where I met my wife, Donna. It's where we raised a family. It's where I built my reputation working with the city's professional teams. It's where I mentored some hard-working, teenage groundskeepers. And it's how I came to work at the first 57 Super Bowls.

Those Super Bowls allowed me to meet people such as Paul McCartney, Lady Gaga, Diana Ross and Garth Brooks. Believe it or not, they're basically ordinary people with extraordinary talents. Good people with a common touch.

I also got to know commissioners, owners, attorneys, sports executives, coaches, players, umpires and fellow groundskeepers. Many became friends. They busted my chops, and I busted theirs – and then some. These are some of the most competitive people in the world, so you have to hold your ground. I may be 5-foot-5, but I didn't back down from any of them. We built a mutual respect.

The Super Bowl has given me some of the highest highs and lowest lows in my professional career. The lows almost killed me.

When I visited my doctors after Super Bowl LVII in 2023, they could tell something didn't seem right.

I had gotten into a deep depression.

What bothered me?

The vocation I had poured my life into had just been exposed on the biggest stage in professional sports.

Players slipping on the field. Players having to change cleats. Players not having the traction to stop a defensive lineman from going around them or cut with a wide receiver.

This wasn't a preseason game. This was Super Bowl LVII.

For 57 of those years – every Super Bowl from Jan. 15, 1967, in Los Angeles to Feb. 12, 2023, in Glendale, Ariz. – I had either been head field supervisor or served as a consultant.

The first 40 Super Bowls went seamlessly for the most part. Whether the games were played on natural grass, poly turf, Astro turf, field turf, matrix turf, sport turf or Tifway, we had few issues.

But problems began with Super Bowl XLI in 2007. Jim Steeg, who ran the NFL's special events from 1979 to 2005, stepped down a couple of years earlier. When Jim left the NFL after Super Bowl XXXIX, there were three people who replaced him. Jim Steeg was that valuable.

For most of the next 17 years, men such as the Kansas City Chiefs' Travis Hogan, the Arizona Cardinals' Andy Levy, Vermont's Lee Keller, myself and others saved the NFL's ass time after time. We kept The Shield from taking some dents and dings.

Those who replaced Jim, my son Chip and me after I stepped aside didn't seem to have the same communication with their superiors. They also didn't communicate well with all the groundskeepers who worked the Super Bowl. Even though I remained as a consultant, it seemed like many felt I was in charge. I often butted heads with those running the show. As the years went by, my concerns were listened to but rarely acted on.

This led to a number of problems with Super Bowl practice and game fields. Groundskeepers aired their grievances to me. I had several meetings with NFL leadership in the stands before Super Bowls. That accomplished little.

I also wrote several letters to NFL Commissioner Roger Goodell. I specifically asked the league to review its approach and work to achieve safer playing fields. Responses I received went from, "We're working on it," to silence. For months.

The responses frustrated the hell out of me. I had built some strong relationships. I truly like Roger Goodell. He has treated me well. But the people he hired weren't getting the job done. And Roger listened to me less and less.

Issues that I kept bringing up with the NFL landed on its doorstep big time in Super Bowl LVII. Besides the Philadelphia Eagles being unhappy with the practice field, a mounting problem reached its worst point when players constantly slipped on the field at State Farm Stadium in Glendale, Ariz., in the world championship game between the Eagles and Kansas City Chiefs.

Fans questioned my integrity. Because I had worked for the Chiefs, Philadelphia fans said I made the field that way to slow down the Eagles' pass rush.

They also criticized groundskeepers and turf company employees who didn't deserve to be criticized.

From the day I started this business, I had a core value: To make the fields I worked on as safe as humanly possible. I've always said the best insurance for the ballplayers is a safe playing field.

Not too slippery so players wouldn't pull muscles. No divots that could lead to ankle injuries. No bad seams on artificial turf that could tear ligaments.

We have good, hard-working groundskeepers such as Andy Levy who truly want to do right by the players. Andy has a conscience.

"These are things that keep me up at night," he said. "The field I prepare for every Sunday home game, there's a half a billion dollars in inventory, human assets. We need to do whatever we can. If I don't do everything to the best it can be, it affects generations. If a quarterback busts his knee and only plays two years, his kids, grandkids and great-grandkids are going to feel that.

"I have a friend who is a doctor. It can be so overwhelming. If I mess up, it's national news. If my doctor friend messes up, somebody could die."

Our staff members would get on their hands and knees for all 57,600 square feet of a football field and make sure every piece of sod was firm. On artificial turf, we made sure every seam was stitched right and clean. We also brushed or raked those fields.

Whether I ran the show as field supervisor or was acting as a consultant, I felt I was responsible. I'm a fixer. I subscribe to a work ethic explained best by former coach Vince Lombardi, who famously said, "You don't do things right once in a while, you do them right all the time."

The lack of response started to affect my health – and sanity. It's ironic because I've told some friends that when I die, I want the NFL shield put over my heart. It means that much to me.

My pay had been reduced to a stipend, but more than the money, I felt I had to walk away or I'd walk into a coffin.

It amazes many – groundskeepers, coaches, referees, players, the players' union, fans – that the NFL would want pristine fields for its exhibition, regular-season and playoff games, only to have a subpar surface for its biggest game of the year.

The sense I've gotten from many I've talked to is that the Super Bowl's halftime show is more important to the NFL than the game itself.

In November 2023, The Athletic's beat writers surveyed 85 players. In the ongoing grass vs. turf debate, nearly 83 percent of the players said NFL playing fields were a real concern.

The NFL continues to grow in popularity. There are 38 million fans alone in South America, Commissioner Roger Goodell said.

The NFL also continues to grow in profitability. In the 2022 season, the NFL made almost $11.9 billion, which was included in the Green Bay Packers' financial statement, released July 20, 2023. As the NFL's only publicly owned franchise, the Packers disclose their expenses and revenues each year along with the league's.

Meanwhile, this year's Super Bowl became the most-watched United States telecast of all time, according to estimates from Nielsen. Its total of 123.7 million viewers was 8 million more than who watched in 2023 when the Chiefs edged the Eagles 38-35.

It ate at me that my final game as a consultant, in my professional opinion, was played on a flawed field.

I guess there's a saying that if it didn't end badly, it wouldn't end at all.

That's why I'm writing this book: to tell my side of the story so we can learn from these missteps and hopefully prevent these situations from ever happening again.

The game field for Super Bowl LVIII in Las Vegas was perfectly manicured, so I felt redeemed in that the pleas of the groundskeepers and me were finally heard.

Over my long career, I've seen many victories and defeats on the fields I prepared for competition. It's been an honor to have played a role in many of America's greatest games.

But before the first pitch or opening kickoff, much work is required of any groundskeeper. As such, I want to take you behind the scenes of my life to illustrate how sports and sports field management have evolved. I hope to shine a spotlight on the work that is completed in the shadows by groundskeepers.

After all, having a safe playing field still is the best insurance for players.

1

Coal Miner's Son

"All creation is a mine,
and every man, a miner."

– Abraham Lincoln

If not for baseball, I wouldn't be alive.

The places I called home – Edwardsville and Wilkes-Barre in Pennsylvania – grew rapidly in the 19th century because nearby coal reserves had been discovered and this drew hundreds of thousands of immigrants, who provided a local labor force. It became known as the anthracite coal region.

My grandparents were among those immigrants. As far back as we can trace my family lineage, they came from Lithuania, Russia, Ukraine, Belgrade and either Bulgaria or Romania. It's hard to know for sure as borders in those countries changed in the 1800s and early 1900s.

A few miles away from Edwardsville and Wilke-Barre was Plymouth, where my dad, George P. Toma Sr., was born. His future would be in those coal mines, and it appeared that it would be my future, too.

In 1929, I was born on Feb. 2, Groundhog Day.

In the Pennsylvania Dutch superstition, if a groundhog emerges from its burrow on this day and sees its shadow, it'll retreat to its den.

Me? There was no retreat, no going back to sleep. I worked. I worked before I was 10, and I'd work into my 90s.

I worked because my family worked. That's what we did.

A couple of miles away from Edwardsville was Kingston, where my mother, Mary, walked every day to work at the Blue Ribbon Bakery. One time, people had to pull my 5-foot mother out of a snow drift.

About the same time that I, George P. Toma Jr., entered the world, Wilkes-Barre's population reached a high of 86,000.

Hard times soon followed.

First came The Great Depression, which lasted from 1929 to 1941. After World War II (1939-45), the city's economy declined due to the collapse of the mining industry.

My father was a breaker in the mines as well as a miner. A breaker cracks the coal into different sizes. I remember him taking me up to the mines and showing me what he did. They had these crushers that broke up the coal. Scared the shit out of me.

My father was a good man. He spent time with me on weekends. He also was a carpenter, made toys for us, was a good cook and took care of my mother.

My dad never complained, but he had serious health challenges. Besides a bad leg, he had been in the hospital for a condition called silicosis. Black lung disease. Medically, it's known as an occupational pneumoconiosis caused by the inhalation of crystalline silica dust. All those years of working in the mines, breathing in that dust, did him in. And did him in at an early age.

My dad died in front of me. My face is the last one he saw on earth. We had returned from a walk. As he came in the front door, he fell. He died in the parlor. July 20, 1940. He was just 46. And I was 11.

Besides my hard-working mother, we had a lot of family members who lent wonderful support to me and my sister,

Catherine. I'd call them angels.

Aunt Eva and Uncle Jay Yarrish. He could speak a dozen languages.

My Uncle Noosh, my mother's brother, who later helped me at Artillery Park.

While dad's death shook me, there wasn't a lot of time to grieve. We needed to put food on the table. We needed to work.

But that's what our Hispanic and Slavic neighbors did. Besides jobs, families had vegetable gardens and also raised cows, chickens, geese and rabbits. The women also swept the porch and gutters.

On vacant lots, we cut the grass, packed it into a coal truck and fed it to our livestock. We also had victory gardens on the coal mine hills. We'd use our pitch forks to loosen the soil.

For a brief time, I lived with my grandmother. Her home was 100 yards from a coal mine. When I think I had it tough, I remember seeing the mules on their rare trips out of the mine. They had cuts and bruises on them from falling rocks.

Grandma's attic had all different types of wild mushrooms we picked, hung on a string and dried. We literally lived off the land. The Great Depression and post-depression times were tough.

But it made me who I am. I have been inducted into eight Hall of Fames, most recently the North American Slavic Hall of Fame. I'm as proud of that honor as any I received.

Father figures mentored me and helped me chart a career. Before my dad died, I started working on a chicken and vegetable farm. I tell my children, grandchildren and great-grandchildren I made 10 cents an hour, 10 hours a day at age 10. Every Saturday, farmer Mike Kuzma told me I could kill two chickens and take them and as many eggs and vegetables as I could carry back to my family. That's why we always ate better on the weekends.

Farmer Mike also taught me an important lesson about leadership. If your team of horses goes into a ditch, you can't just prod the lazy one, you have to prod the harder-working one.

Same thing for a head groundskeeper. I had to drive my workers. This could be done sternly, or this could be done with a kind word. Either way, before they went home, the job needed to be finished.

There was time for playing sports, but we had to improvise. For a football, we used rags that we taped together. For basketball, we used Carnation milk cans and poles. The hoop was a five-gallon metal milk can. For baseball, we used broomsticks for bats. The balls were rags bound with tape.

I kept my chin up, even though times were tough while growing up in a coal region.

I remember building a pitching mound. The field was rough, but we overcame that by taking springs from worn-out mattresses and dragging them around to smooth the playing area.

Standing only 5-foot-5, I felt my chances as a big-time ballplayer were slim. However, years later, I learned from Kansas City Royals shortstop Fred Patek that height didn't make might. Freddie played in the majors from 1968 to 1981 despite being 5-5.

However, I knew I wanted to be involved in sports in some way. I also loved the idea of taking the land, the earth, the soil and molding it.

Some call it a baseball field, others call it a baseball diamond. And what is a diamond but a rock, a mineral. Like coal, it is found in mines deep below the earth's surface. Diamonds are the hardest natural material on earth but when cut – by other diamonds – and polished, they become a thing of beauty.

Diamonds may be a girl's best friend, but baseball diamonds became one of my best friends. They helped open doors to a wonderful career that gave me the chance to meet some of sports' and entertainment's most talented and powerful people.

Not bad for a depression-era kid who lost his dad before becoming a teenager in coal-mining country.

I knew what I wanted to do even as a teenager.

2

Eight-Decade Career Begins

"Every blade of grass has an angel that bends over it and whispers, 'Grow, grow, grow.' "

– From the Talmud, a central text of Rabbinic Judaism and the primary source of Jewish religious law and Jewish theology

I don't know if Stan Schlecker, our neighbor, noticed our primitive way of dragging an infield.

But I do remember him taking us to ball games at Artillery Park when he was the groundskeeper for the Wilkes-Barre Barons.

Artillery Park hosted some of the game's greatest players, including Babe Ruth, who smashed a home run that was estimated at 650 feet in a 1926 exhibition game.

Among the players and managers who represented Wilkes-Barre while I worked there were Hall of Famers Tony Lazzeri and Bob Lemon as well as five-time World Series champion Lefty Gomez, Mike Garcia, Joe Tipton and Johnny Blatnik.

Mr. Schlecker hired me and Jimmy Mazzlo, an Italian

boy, when I was 13 in 1942. The United States was in World War II by then.

That started my 80 years as a groundskeeper. Staff member Ben McNally and secretary Helen Tomasick also helped me.

Grounds crew members Henry Golightly and Raymond Hayward would follow me on future stops.

A heavyset man, Mr. Schlecker would bring me lunch, then take me to a little grocery store his wife operated. He was like a father to me.

My first jobs as assistant groundskeeper included leveling the infield dirt, matting it and getting the baselines right. I also fixed the pitching mound and used a push lawn mower to cut the infield grass.

Right across from the right-field gate at Artillery Park was a Wilkes-Barre Parks Department maintenance shop with lawn mowers and tractors in the back. When the workers took a break for lunch, they gave me a tractor, which I used to cut the outfield grass and sidelines.

I also played janitor. Jimmy and I swept the stands and cleaned under the bleachers. We also had to clean the one men's and one women's bathroom in the park.

While I watched over the field during games, Jimmy ran the scoreboard. He was faster than the umpires on balls and strikes.

When Bill Veeck became owner of the Cleveland Indians in 1946, he also became the Barons' new owner. After changing the franchise's Class A team name to Indians, he hired me as his new head groundskeeper. Stan Schlecker, who helped guide me, was promoted to head trainer and bus driver.

"A good groundskeeper is worth five to seven victories a season," Mr. Veeck always would say.

To show how much he thought of me and the profession, Mr. Veeck sent me to work with Emil Bossard.

Working with Emil would turn out to be one of the great learning experiences in my life. Call it an internship or a

Artillery Park in Wilkes-Barre, Pa., where I got my start.

college education, here I was being trained by the best groundskeeper who has ever done it.

I learned so much from the man, and I quickly applied many of his ideas. He became my mentor, and I constantly asked for his advice.

Emil taught me to think outside the box. For example, in 1948, the Wilkes-Barre Parks Department didn't have any equipment to till up the infield dirt. So I called on a local farmer, and he lent me one mule and one harrow, a farm implement used for surface tillage.

And when I sent the Indians the farmer's bill of $25, I wrote down "Mule rental."

We also got some natural fertilizer out of the deal.

In later years, we would get some of our best cow manure from England, though we had to stop when there was an outbreak of Mad Cow Disease.

One of the umpires who worked at Artillery Park was Nestor Chylak, a fellow Ukrainian who lived 18 miles up the road. Mr. Chylak went on to work Major League Baseball games from 1954 to 1978. He worked six all-star games and five World Series and played a role in two games being declared forfeits because of fan riots that left the fields unplayable and unsafe.

I had to take a break from groundskeeping when I was drafted and served our country in the Korean War from December of 1950 until spring 1953.

After going to leadership school at Fort Knox in Kentucky and Fort Sill in Oklahoma, I was a staff sergeant for the 2nd Infantry Division, "Indianhead," with the 32nd battalion.

We had six men operating a 105mm howitzer. I learned a valuable lesson on the importance of teamwork.

We backed up the French and Turkish military. The Turks liked to fight hand-to-hand combat, which often was at night.

We found the Chinese to be resilient. We'd knock out a Chinese outpost one day, and the next day it would be put up again.

It was a rough war. Almost 37,000 Americans died. However, it wasn't as bad as the 58,000 lives lost in Vietnam and the 400,000 lost in World War II.

I felt like I returned to Wilkes-Barre a changed man.

War will do that to you.

Returning Home

I quickly followed new opportunities, but over the years, I never forgot my hometown roots.

I always returned to see my mother and sister around Christmas. The year my first son, Ryan, was born, we went to Pennsylvania to have him baptized at St. Vladimir's, the Ukrainian church.

We were gone for five days, around baseball's all-star break, and that was one of the longest vacations I took.

In August of 2022, I had quite a weekend when I returned to my hometown. I was featured in an interview on WBRE TV Channel 28, and had newspaper interviews with both the Times Leader and Citizen's Voice. Lastly, I was featured in a four-page layout in Happenings Magazine, telling about my interesting journey.

Wilkes-Barre mayor George Brown presented me with a key to the city at the Wyoming Valley Challenger Baseball Little League field. I reminded their staff led by Dan Mulhern that every child deserves a "safe" place to play and grow. I told them that this was one of the finest ballfields that I have ever seen, for this level. Next, Edwardsville mayor Sherri Dubaskas Cordes and the Borough Council also presented me with a proclamation, to honor me.

Then finally, the Luzerne County Sports Hall of Fame inducted me into its 38th Class for its Hall of Fame ceremony. This nonprofit organization has a banquet annually, which helps to raise money for a number of worthy causes in a five-county area of northeastern Pennsylvania.

At the banquet, when I was introduced as the next Hall of Famer to speak, those in attendance wouldn't stop clapping for me in a standing ovation, until president Jim Martin told them to have a seat, allowing me to tell my story. I began by saying, "I come from a valley with a heart."

Jim has such a great knowledge and passion for the local athletes and coaches as well as those who have had an impact on sports in Luzerne County. He knows I was born on Swallow Street. Under his watch, he was able to help rewrite the history books, when his research uncovered a granddaughter to Red Grange that no one knew about. One of the NFL's greatest early stars, Grange was born in Forksville, Pa. in Sullivan County, in 1903.

I'm spoiled when I visit and give Jim a call. He brings me some of my favorite Polish foods, takes me to Patte's restaurant and then takes me to the ball fields. Jim's goal is to dedicate an area adjacent to Artillery Park, in my honor. Since I live on a street called Terrace in my hometown, Jim presented the city with an idea to place a seated memorial area in Kirby Park, next to where I got my start. It would be called, "Toma Terrace."

"Every ball field has a terrace," Jim said. "The picture in my mind is of a seating area with an overhang, where everyone is having a cool drink, and feeling comfortable while watching a ballgame. People will be able to sit there and remember the ballfield, and the boys of summer.

"George never will be forgotten. I'll do this before I leave as president."

Moving Up In The Minors

My work in Wilkes-Barre started to get me noticed in the baseball world, thanks to Bill Veeck.

After the war, I started working for the Detroit Tigers, who were outstanding with John McHale and Jim Campbell. The two, who would go on to have distinguished careers in baseball, treated me like a son.

In 1955, the Tigers made me their head groundskeeper at Triple-A Buffalo. I enjoyed working with Danny Carnevale, who later became a manager for many clubs. Hillman Lyons and Bob Steinhilper were outstanding.

When the Tigers sold the Buffalo franchise, then moved to Charleston, W.Va., in 1956, I followed.

My next stop? Everybody, including me, assumed it would be the New York Yankees.

Between 1936 and 1964 the Yankees won 16 world championships while appearing in 22 World Series. The Montreal Canadiens are the only other professional team to have gone on that kind of run.

My Yankees offer came in 1957. I would start by working with the team's Triple-A affiliate in Denver. The feeling was after getting that experience, I'd get my call-up to the majors. Yankee Stadium. However, another job became available with the Kansas City Athletics.

The choice seemed easy. The best team in the majors vs. the worst team in the majors.

The Yankees could pay more and offer more resources.

Meanwhile, Kansas City's situation seemed dire. Other respectable groundskeepers had tried – and failed. Even Emil Bossard discouraged me from taking the job.

"George, don't go (to Kansas City)," he said. "I worked there a couple of times for (manager) Lou Boudreau. In the spring, the rains flood you out, and in the summer, the heat bakes you out."

Then I received another perspective from a friend who said, "George, the best thing for you to do is to go to Kansas City. If you screw up, nobody will notice it's so bad."

But as I spoke with various mentors, colleagues and baseball people, a thought came into my mind:

What if I succeeded? What if I made the field the class of the majors?

Flying back from Daytona Beach, Fla., after the Cleveland Indians' spring training in 1950 with Mr. Perry (left), who was the general manager in Wilkes-Barre, Pa.

3

Kansas City Here I Come

I shall be telling this with a sigh
Somewhere ages and ages hence:
Two roads diverged in a wood, and I –
I took the one less traveled by,
And that has made all the difference.

– Robert Frost, The Road Not Taken

In 1952, Jerry Leiber and Mike Stoller wrote "Kansas City." It became a chart-topping hit when Wilbert Harrison recorded it in 1959.

Leiber and Stoller were 19-year-old students from Los Angeles. The duo never had visited Kansas City before writing that song.

Neither had I when I came to the City of Fountains for an interview in 1957. I went to Denver after that, on a Monday, for another interview with Bob Howsam and his brother Earl. They represented the New York Yankees.

As ballclubs, the Yankees and Kansas City Athletics showed the disparity of Major League Baseball.

The Yankees had just won their 17th world championship

in 1956. The Athletics never had a winning season in their 13 years in Kansas City from 1955 to 1967.

There's a good reason for this. For the first half of their time in K.C., the Athletics basically were the New York Yankees' farm team, a story well written by Jeff Katz in *The Kansas City A's & the Wrong Half of the Yankees*. The two teams made a whopping 16 trades from 1955 to 1960, most of them one-sided.

On their way to the American League pennant in 1957, the Yankees' regulars included Mickey Mantle, Yogi Berra, Bill Skowron, Bobby Richardson, Andy Carey, Gil McDougald, Enos Slaughter and Hank Bauer.

The Athletics' regulars included Vic Power, Billy Hunter, Hector Lopez, Joe DeMaestri, Guz Zernial, Woodie Held, Lou Skizas and Hal Smith.

Zernial, Power and Smith were the only players among the Kansas City regulars who never played for the Yankees. Each of the other eight players either had played for the Yankees before playing for the Athletics or would play for the Yankees in the future.

New York also hired good upper-management people.

Bob Howsam would later become general manager of the St. Louis Cardinals (1964-67) when they won a World Series in '64, and his moves helped the Cards win another title in '67 and return to the World Series in 1968. His run as Cincinnati Reds GM (1967-77) resulted in two World Series titles and four National League pennants.

Howsam took care of the little people. When we talked about the possibility of me working for the Yankees, I asked the ballplayers, "What if I don't want to live in New York?"

The players said, "George, you can live in Teaneck."

When I said that would require me to pay 50 cents to go over the George Washington Bridge, the Yankees players said, "They'll pay you $500 a month for bridge fare."

I'd be making money on that deal. Plus, the Yankees offered much more pay than Kansas City.

However, I instantly fell in love with Kansas City and the

people. And I still love K.C. I suffered financially in the short term, and I suffered financially in the long term.

And it was a bad, bad field. But I liked challenges.

The Toma Touch

The groundskeepers who preceded me were good, but their backgrounds were more with golf courses. They didn't know how to take care of a baseball field, particularly an infield.

Because the previous groundskeeper didn't have enough help, he and his men couldn't put the tarp on the field. When he cut it in half, he was fired.

When I first saw the Municipal Stadium field, built in 1923, there were more weeds than there was grass. I noticed crabgrass, crowfoot grass. When we sprayed the field to kill the weeds, the grass browned.

The dirt also was bad.

The Athletics also were so cheap all they provided was a Toro professional mower, an aerifier and an International tractor. We had to sell broken seats and cardboard from the concession stands to Cohen's junkyard to get money to buy seed at Rudy Patrick Seed Company.

At first, fans heckled me like they did the players. They knew my background. "Ah, send him back to Charleston," they said.

So how did we resurrect the field? We laid down rye grass in March, April and May. We then started Bermuda seed on Memorial Day. By July 4, the seeds took to the hot weather. We also laid down bio-stimulants – a fancy name for cow manure – to make the grass grow.

We soon had an oasis in the desert.

The infield dirt came from Mrs. Zimmerman's farm, a combination of Marshall loam and No. 8 plaster sand from the nearby Kaw River. Coincidentally, it was in Edwardsville. Edwardsville, Kansas.

I soon added other touches. In 1960, I dressed up the batting circles with the insignias of the A's and the visiting club. Other groundskeepers started to copy me. I also installed French drains for better drainage and improved the water system.

When the Athletics played host to a Major League Baseball All-Star Game in 1960, I received great feedback on the field. Wilkes-Barre writer Lou Rauscher noted how the hometown boy was doing well.

Charles O. Finley

Charles O. Finley needed to wait six years to buy the Kansas City Athletics. He wanted to buy the franchise from the Philadelphia Athletics in 1954, but Major League Baseball owners approved Arnold Johnson.

In 1936, the Kansas City Blues were the top affiliate of the New York Yankees. From 1936 to 1954, the Blues won three American Association championships. They moved to Denver when Johnson moved the Athletics to K.C. in 1955. He sold Blues Stadium to the city, which renamed it Municipal Stadium.

The Athletics still seemed like the Yankees' little brother when Johnson approved so many deals that gave a strong appearance that the Yankees were robbing the Athletics. There were a lot of rumors that Johnson and the Yanks were colluding. Even owner Bill Veeck said in John Peterson's book *The Kansas City Athletics, A Baseball History 1954-1967* that the A's were "nothing more than a loosely controlled Yankee farm club."

After Johnson died in March of 1960 while watching the team in spring training, Mr. Finley bought a controlling interest in the Kansas City Athletics from Johnson's estate. He bought out minority owners a year later. He also brought in his cousin Carl in 1962 to look over the fine print on contracts, according to Carl's daughter, Nancy Finley.

While Carl had to live in the city where the team was located, he also had the right to veto any potential move if he didn't want to live in the new city. Few people knew about that. His daughter did.

While Mr. Finley never finished college – and felt insecure

Kansas City Athletics owner Charles Finley, left, and I got along great in my early days in Kansas City.

about it – Carl had a degree in history and a master's in journalism and law.

Although he didn't have a winning season in Kansas City, Mr. Finley did his best to make the Athletics better. Called by Marvin Miller, MLB players union founder, "absolutely the best judge of baseball talent I've ever seen," Mr. Finley started to bring in talented players such as pitchers Catfish Hunter and Rollie Fingers, shortstop Bert Campaneris and third baseman Sal Bando.

The A's also drafted Rick Monday in 1965, Hall of Famer Reggie Jackson in 1966 and star lefty Vida Blue in 1967. The A's traded Monday a few years later for pitcher Ken Holtzman.

While he had talented people such as farm director Hank Peters – who later helped the Baltimore Orioles have six seasons of 90 wins or more – Mr. Finley was general manager. He limited his deals with the Yankees like in past years.

When the Yankees and their 296-foot right field was grandfathered in, Finley installed his own 296-foot right field. Right behind it were stands called the "K.C. Pennant Porch." When a 1958 MLB rule passed that no new major-league fence could be closer than 325 feet, Mr. Finley had to move the fences back.

He tried to get even by having a white line painted on the field of the original "K.C. Pennant Porch" distance, then have the announcer say, "That would have been a home run in Yankee Stadium." However, the announcer stopped after the Athletics' foes hit more balls in that area.

I think Mr. Finley also liked me because I stayed with Kansas City despite overtures from the franchise he hated.

He told Rex Lardner of Sports Illustrated that I was the best in baseball while adding, "The Yankees are trying to get him away from me, but they won't."

While portrayed as wanting to move the Athletics, Charlie often bluffed, Nancy Finley said. Some of the places he talked about moving to – Peculiar, Mo.; Normal, Ill. – were small towns. He just wanted a lease agreement equal to the $1 a year the city gave Kansas City Chiefs owner Lamar Hunt.

Kansas City officials gave Finley a favorable lease agreement for a while, but it didn't last. Attendance dipped.

Finley finally took up Oakland officials on their offer and moved the Athletics west in 1968. Not even the Missouri governor giving Mr. Finley a Missouri mule helped. Mr. Finley loved mules.

A few years later, the Athletics won World Series titles in 1972, 1973 and 1974. The Kansas City Royals, an expansion franchise established in 1969 after the Athletics relocated, finished second to the A's in the American League's West Division in '73.

Alvin Dark, who had managed in Kansas City, led the A's

to their title in '74. Two years later, most of the Oakland stars left via free agency.

While Finley has an awful reputation in baseball, I loved the guy. He treated me well, and he treated the crew well.

Besides doubling our salaries, he once paid me for six months and told me he didn't want to see me at Municipal Stadium or he'd fire me. Then he paused and said, "That won't work. If I see you at the stadium, I'll fire our security guard."

Nancy Finley said Charles O. Finley spent $500,000 to renovate Municipal Stadium. He also loved to promote. A mechanical rabbit, Harvey, popped out of the grass and brought baseballs to the umpires.

In a season opener, Finley had all kinds of birds put inside Harvey. When the umpires opened the ball compartment, the fleeing birds shit on them and A's catcher Haywood Sullivan. It must have been good luck. Sullivan hit a walk-off homer to win the game.

Mr. Finley also had a pitch clock on the pitcher, nearly 60 years before Major League Baseball instituted it as a rule. He was able to book a date for the Beatles to come to Municipal Stadium in 1964 and paid a whopping $150,000 ($1.4 million today).

In left field, we had a picnic grounds where fans sat in the shade with 10 sugar maple trees blocking out the sun. In right field, there were carriage lights that illuminated at night.

Mr. Finley had a dog he called Old Drum, based on the legendary hound in the late 1860s who was shot and killed because it was thought he had killed the neighbors' sheep. Old Drum's owner took the neighbors to court in Warrensburg, Missouri, and won.

We also had a literal zoo in left field for little children with sheep grazing, pheasants and rabbits running around, a shepherd – Tom Weakley, who appeared on the TV show *What's My Line?* – and, of course, the mule, Charlie-O.

And monkeys, which Mr. Finley named after his uncles. Oh, did they create havoc.

When Mo Hayward cleaned their cage, they took cigarettes

out of his pocket. When the monkeys unlocked the cages and ran away, we had to try and catch them with butterfly nets.

But we didn't catch them all. One lady called and said there was a monkey in her garage. When we read of a monkey found in Columbia, Mo. – 125 miles away – we figured one got on a freight train and went for a ride.

The visiting Detroit Tigers' players had fun with the monkeys. They filled a hypodermic needle with vodka, then shot it into oranges before feeding the oranges to the monkeys. Then, they just watched as the monkeys got drunk.

Charlie-O was treated the best. His pen was immaculate. Bob Johnson, who rode War Paint in Kansas City Chiefs games, also took care of the mule. Charles O. Finley had a special trailer made with music for his mule where he took him to American League cities.

If the hotel barkeepers allowed the mule to have a beer in their establishment, the players stayed in the hotel. If they didn't, Finley moved them to another hotel.

When he couldn't sneak Charley-O into Comiskey Park, he had him shipped there.

Ever the innovative promoter, Athletics owner Charles Finley sits on his mule, Charlie-O., in the lobby of a New York hotel.

He also made player – and later broadcaster – Ken "Hawk" Harrelson ride his mule. Harrelson hated that.

Somehow, Mr. Finley also got Charlie-O inside a New York hotel. There are pictures to prove it.

When Finley announced he was taking his team to Oakland, I made myself scarce. I knew if he saw me, he'd be able to talk me into going with him.

Harvey the mechanical rabbit went with Mr. Finley to Oakland but sat in a cage because I wasn't there to take care of him, Nancy said.

Still, I went to Oakland to take care of his field occasionally. Didn't charge him a penny. In return, he gave the kids – Chip and Rick – money gifts. Rick – who fought in Desert Storm – received $1,000 at birth for a college education.

Mr. Finley also gave me a wonderful gift after the A's won their third straight World Series title – a World Series ring. The ring had a green diamond as well as a three-leaf clover to commemorate the titles in '72, '73 and '74.

The ring had the letter "S" inscribed on it three times to represent "sweat plus sacrifice equals success."

When Mr. Finley returned to town, I'd meet him for dinner. Sometimes, I wonder if the Royals had a problem with me being so close to Charles O. Finley. All I can say is they didn't treat me nearly as well as Mr. Finley did.

Powerful Encounters

In the late 1960s, I had a couple of face-to-face meetings with two powerful men – Orioles manager Hank Bauer and evangelist Billy Graham.

A former Kansas City Athletics player, Hank helped the Yankees win seven World Series. For years, he held the postseason record with hits in 17 straight games.

Later, the Yankees traded him for Roger Maris. Another bad deal for the Athletics.

Hank and I had become good friends. He also tried to get me to come to the Yankees when he played there.

He also suspected the Athletics of cheating – and he was

right. But he didn't find out from me. I'm no stoolie.

Hank and I took a walk over to the outfield fence. When he started asking me what certain wires were for with the scoreboard, I told him they were for Kansas City Chiefs football. This wire was for the time clock, that wire was for the second clock, and that wire was for the scoreboard clock.

What we had was a large light tower with a Butternut Bread sign. Two dots lighted meant a fastball, and one dot was a breaking pitch. We also used a lantern light in Charlie-O's pen.

Five years later, Hank found out from someone that his suspicions of the Athletics cheating were correct.

So, he invited me to a restaurant, nice as could be. When I arrived, he was all over my ass.

In 1967, evangelist Billy Graham had a 10-day crusade at Municipal Stadium.

To give you a little background, Graham, a Southern Baptist minister, was the most well-known preacher of his time. He spoke on television and at crusades for six decades. Millions watched or attended. He spoke all over the world and had the ear of American presidents. I'm not sure we will see anyone like him again.

Vocally opposed to racism, Billy Graham joined with Martin Luther King for a revival in New York City in 1957. When he visited South Africa and spoke at a rally before 100,000, the first mixed-race event, he said, "Apartheid is a sin."

We became good friends, and during his event, I asked him if he could avoid kneeling on the grass. He complied.

It didn't matter.

The first few nights, there weren't enough people to fill the stands.

But on a Sunday afternoon, people kept coming. Bumper-to-bumper traffic. They came from miles away.

First I said, "Please, keep them off the grass."

Then I said, "OK, let them go to left field."

Then I said, "OK, let them go to right field."

Finally, I said, "OK, put them on the grass in the infield."

People sat everywhere but on the dirt because they wore their Sunday finery.

It was a great crusade. I met singer Johnny Cash and his wife June Carter Cash. They sat in the first row, then came up to the stage and sang. Johnny Cash and his wife came to many of Billy Graham's crusades.

The grass took a beating. However, I told Paul Kirk of the Kansas City Star, "Maybe the Lord will take care of us because we took such good care of Billy Graham."

Later, Mr. Graham and Mr. Cash had a get-together at Excelsior Springs, Mo. They invited me.

The most amazing thing at the crusade? One night, they collected a lot of money, a big basket of money. Then someone left the basket on the altar stage all night.

Nobody stole it.

Billy Graham returned to Kansas City in 1978 and 2004. He died in 2018 at the age of 99. He was quite a man.

Get Off My Lawn

In 1962, Lamar Hunt looked to move his professional football team from Dallas to Kansas City.

When he arrived, we got off to a bad start – and it was my doing. I was working on the roof of a storage shed behind center field at Municipal Stadium. There was a hole in the roof where the flagpole stood, so in the fall and winter, I covered the hole with plywood.

While I worked, a man started walking across the field. I didn't allow that unless he was a player.

I proceeded to slide down the flagpole like a fireman, ran onto the field, yelled at the man and told him to get off the field.

About an hour later, I was re-introduced to Mr. Hunt along with Dallas Texans president Jack Steadman by the mayor of Kansas City, H. Roe Bartle.

A bit embarrassed, I now had to give Mr. Hunt and Mr. Steadman the grand tour of Municipal Stadium – playing field, press boxes, team offices, clubhouses, concession stands.

They were scouting a new home for a pro football team. While the Dallas Texans won the AFL championship in 1962, they had a hard time drawing fans because they went up against the Dallas Cowboys.

Mr. Hunt and Mr. Steadman must have liked what they saw because the Dallas Texans became the Kansas City Chiefs.

Known as "Chief," Mayor Bartle insisted on the team being named after him because he was known as "Chief Lone Bear" as part of the Mic-O-Say program with the Boy Scouts.

It's actually a great trivia question because many people think the team's nickname comes from Native Americans. That fact played a role in why the Kansas City Chiefs haven't had to change their nickname like the Cleveland Indians and Washington Redskins.

A month after he moved the team, Mr. Hunt told me I'd keep my position. We not only joked about the incident, but he admired my tenacity.

"That guy's so tough, so particular, I want him working for me," Mr. Hunt said.

And by continuing to maintain the field for football games, I would be given my biggest professional opportunity.

4

Scramble Drill

"Age is a case of mind over matter.
If you don't mind, it don't matter."

– Satchel Paige

I've made so many friends and gotten to know so many people throughout my travels around the country and around the world, but there are few relationships I've had that can equal my interactions with the black groundskeepers and the black community in Kansas City.

I believe I have a close bond with them because when I needed help early in my career, they were always there. Always. When we had to work long hours, they were there. When we had to sleep at the stadium, they were there.

And over the last six decades, when I needed to talk to someone, they were there. We've remained close, which makes me feel really good. They're the epitome of being treasured friends – and then some.

Kansas City has a rich baseball tradition, which includes the Negro Leagues. The Kansas City Monarchs won 62 percent of their games as well as two World Series (1924, 1942) and

13 National and American league titles while playing 37 seasons in the Negro Leagues (1920-30, 1937-62).

Their top players are legends – Buck O'Neil, Satchel Paige, James "Cool Papa" Bell, Jackie Robinson and Ernie Banks – as well as Turkey Stearnes, Newt Allen, Jesse Williams and Bonnie Serrell.

Buck O'Neil became a great friend and an absolutely wonderful ambassador for Major League Baseball. Just watch Ken Burns' incredible documentary *Baseball.* Buck's voice and stories were used regularly throughout the nine-part series.

On Sept. 25, 1965, Kansas City Athletics owner Charles O. Finley brought Satchel Paige out of retirement after 12 years. Before the game, writer Mike Huber wrote that when Finley asked Paige, then 59, if he could pitch three innings, he replied, "That depends. How many times a day?"

Ole Satch pitched three scoreless innings against the Boston Red Sox.

Former Kansas City Royals star Frank White, who attended the game, said, "We loved baseball. It was America's game, plus the stadium was in the heart of our neighborhood. I lived seven blocks away from the stadium. We lived three blocks away from Satchel, and I went to school with his kids.

"People would park in people's yards, and they'd watch the cars. Everybody loved baseball."

A graduate of the Royals Academy, Frank was appointed county executive by the Jackson County Legislature in 2016.

Much-Needed Help

When I arrived in Kansas City, one of the first people who helped me was Henry Wheat, a great man who later would become maintenance manager at Kauffman Stadium.

One night we did all we could to put a tarp on the field. Now, I tell you, when you're unwrapping the tarp, you run like hell and hope you don't fall.

The scariest thing around, if you fall, is when the tarp goes over your head. Suddenly, it goes dark, and you wonder if you'll ever see light again. It's like being in a tunnel.

How did we take the tarp off? Henry was able to get $20 from the ticket office. With the ballpark at 22nd and Brooklyn, he went to 18th and Vine – a big jazz district – and recruited 10 winos whom he paid $2 each to take the tarp off.

My first grounds crew at Municipal Stadium included Larry, Kenny, Jimmy and Sugar Chouteau, along with Charles McComber and one outstanding young guy, Frank Meredith.

Frank's father fought in Germany in World War II. After the war, he married a German girl and had Frank. When Frank was 14, he and his grandmother jumped over the Berlin Wall. They nearly were caught but escaped and settled in Kansas City.

When Frank was 16, I sort of adopted and mentored him.

Then there were the high school kids from Lincoln Preparatory Academy and Central High who started helping me in 1962.

They were dedicated, and they were fast. Sid Bordman of the Kansas City Star wrote about the crew.

Because we didn't have automatic irrigation in those days – and didn't until the mid-1990s – my crew often would stay at the stadium all night. They'd sleep either in the dugouts, on top of the batting cages or on top of the net.

Gino Armstrong was captain of the infield raking crew. He was one of the first blacks hired. His brother Gerald was the first black to work in the visiting clubhouse.

The Bruce family – which had 12 children – had all seven of its young men on the crew. If they didn't stay at the stadium, their mother would put them in a cab at 5 a.m. to get them there.

Andre, a great friend of my son Chip, had a distinguished career from 1991 to 2013 leading the Kansas City Chiefs' grounds crew.

Wilford Jr., who started in 1962, became the director of landscaping for the Truman Sports Complex.

Dennis stayed for 15 years after starting in 1969. After that, he started his M&M Lawn Service, which he still owns today. It's one of the largest lawn services in the city.

I used to call Dennis regularly to give him assignments. He worked with me for a handful of Super Bowls as a painter.

Reginald did a little bit of everything – seeding, putting lines down, mowing. He later became a barbecue pit chef, working at Arthur Bryant's for 35 years.

Gregory, who joined in 1964, was deployed to Vietnam during the war and now works in security.

Roland, who started working on the crew at 16, was part of the team during the Royals' 2015 World Series victory.

Elliott, the youngest of the Bruce brothers, began working with the crew in 1985, the year the Royals won their first World Series. When the fans stormed the field, we let them take all the dirt they wanted by the bases, by the pitcher's mound, by home plate. The only thing we didn't allow them to take was the pitching rubber.

I recruited Melvin Duncan at 14 after seeing him at a game. He was among those who helped pull the tarp over the field.

"George said, 'Hey, you,' " Melvin remembered. "I thought he was talking to someone else, but he was talking to me. He asked me to help put the tarp on. Two guys pulled with the rope, and two pushed the tarp.

"Afterwards, he said, 'Take this paper home to have your parents sign.' He also said, 'If you work for me, you gotta go to school.'

"I liked that about him."

Melvin said I was tough but in a good way. He led our scramble drill team because he lived just a block from Municipal Stadium. One of the security guards would call members of the team. When the guard said "Scramble", the youths would rush to the ballpark and help cover the field when it looked like we'd get rain.

With my Scramble Drill guys and three right-hand men that started with me at the old Municipal Stadium. From left to right: Dennis Bruce, football foreman; me; Melvin Duncan, is in charge of the baseball stadium; and Wilford Bruce, landscaping foreman.

Melvin said the ballplayers liked the grounds crew so much they paid them to wash their cars and hid $20 and $100 bills in the Royals' bullpen and foam padding every Sunday thanks to Dan Quisenberry and Amos Otis.

A member of the crew for 14 years, Melvin worked with me when the Royals made the playoffs in the 1970s. He also worked Super Bowl VI in New Orleans in 1972.

"It was one helluva experience," Melvin said.

Melvin Duncan led a group that included Phil Drake, William Davis, Oscar Jones and Kenneth Chouteau, a former Marine who was wounded in Vietnam in 1966. He worked first base.

I told Michael Satchell of the Kansas City Star that watching them work reminded me of the Marines.

"It's strictly a military operation," I said. "It takes discipline, skill and great teamwork."

The crew also earned a reputation for being able to drag the field in 28 seconds. If they had to roll the tarp out for a rainstorm, they could do it in 45 seconds.

Legendary Yankees announcer Mel Allen said, "Those men should be in the Olympics."

Our crew reuniting in 2022. Bottom row: Gregory Bruce, me, Andre Bruce. Middle row: Oscar Jones, Reginold Bruce, Denny Bruce, Wilford Bruce, Roland Bruce. Top row: Melvin Duncan, Nelson Thomas, Elliott Bruce.

The Milwaukee Brewers once challenged our crew to a contest based on dragging the field, touching up the mound and cleaning home plate. My guys didn't lose.

The crew worked fast despite the heat. If you sat in the dugout during those afternoon games, you literally could see the heat waves coming off the field.

The crew and I started to get positive press from ballplayers, media and opposing teams for our work, and it kept improving when Mr. Finley bought the Kansas City Athletics in 1960.

A native of Alabama, Mr. Finley treated me and my grounds crew very well.

Mr. Finley doubled my salary and my crew's salary. Before

games, he'd feed them Kansas City steaks and barbecue from Arthur Bryant's in the picnic area. He'd mingle with the grounds crew, and when they'd sing for him, he'd give them 20 bucks. He also gave them money for school supplies.

Mr. Finley also bragged to Sports Illustrated's Rex Lardner that he had the fastest infield-tarp-unrolling crew in the majors after also beating the Yankees' grounds crew. He added they also had the keenest eyes in baseball when it came to lining the baselines and the batters' boxes.

"The kids are doing a helluva job," Mr. Finley would tell his wife.

When Melvin left, he drove trucks, mostly for the United States Postal Service.

Nelson Thomas started selling popcorn and peanuts in the stands and then was a bat boy before I recommended him to join the grounds crew.

"It was a helluva advancement," Nelson said. "Henry Wheat told me to go to Municipal Stadium and meet with Cedric Tallis. Cedric invited me to his office and offered me the job.

"I was there for Opening Day in 1969. Someone said, 'You're famous.' I said, 'I'll be famous when they pay me.' "

Nelson can confirm he and the crew slept over at the stadium many nights, especially when school was out.

"George would tell us it's gonna be extremely hot, so as soon as the sun came up, we'd give the grass a good watering with a water hose, then at noon, then again at 3 p.m.," Nelson said.

Nelson said he never worked as hard as he did when we converted Municipal Stadium from a baseball ballpark to a football field. He also said he never got as cold as he did for a 1971 playoff game between the Chiefs and Miami Dolphins on Christmas. To this day, it's the longest playoff game in NFL history - 82 minutes, 40 seconds.

"My foot still tingles when somebody mentions that game," Nelson said.

Maybe that's why he went into the music business when we moved to the Truman Sports Complex.

Nelson jokes he went from piano to flutophone to clarinet to saxophone to flute to sousaphone in the marching band. The band performed regularly. He quickly moved on from sousaphone because he couldn't look down, which led to him stepping in horse shit when the band marched during parades.

His travels took him from California to Chicago to Rome, where he played in the Colosseum.

"Our dressing room was in the old lion's den," he said. "It hadn't changed much.

"I went from playing R&B and jazz to a jazz orchestra and avant-garde and swing in Europe."

Even though he worked on the crew for a short time, we kept in touch.

Nelson is one of my biggest fans. He tells people, "George Toma can take a wheat field full of dandelions and make it the best field."

Ewing Kauffman

As much as I liked Charles O. Finley and his support of the grounds crew, I had problems with Royals owner Ewing Kauffman, who didn't seem to value our efforts.

Kauffman is considered a Kansas City hero because he worked with Major League Baseball to bring the game back to the city in 1969, then oversaw the Royals' great run in the 1970s and 1980s.

A billionaire for his investment in pharmaceuticals, Kauffman also contributed to a number of causes in the area with his wife, Muriel.

But Kauffman never treated the grounds crew well. At times, he did compliment me. I wish he had done more of it with my guys.

Most minor-league teams had better equipment than we did. For 35 acres, we had one tractor and one Toro Whirlwind mower.

When a tractor stalled as I cut the grass behind the scoreboard, I cussed. People came out of the stadium clubhouse.

Detroit Tigers legend Norm Cash walked over with another man.

"What's the matter George?" he said.

I said, "We're playing tonight, and here they gave me one tractor, it's a used tractor and it won't start. And they expect me to cut 35 acres. They don't give a shit."

At that moment, Cash introduced me to Hilton Hayes, the district manager for John Deere out of Dallas.

"George, don't worry," he said.

Every year for 10 years, we received a delivery worth $800,000 of new John Deere equipment without being charged a dime. That included snowblowers and grass-cutting machines that had air conditioning in them. Best equipment on the market.

Kaufmann, he never said thank you.

Trevor Vance, the Royals' long-time groundskeeper, had a bobblehead night. He came out on one of those John Deere tractors as part of the promotion.

Following John Deere's lead, other businessmen also gave

We made quite an entrance with the Athletics fire truck.

Me with Trevor Vance, who has been with the Kansas City Royals since 1985.

us grass seed, fertilizer, bio stimulants, herbicides, insecticides, fungicides and sod inside and outside of Kansas City. The gifts came from as far away as England.

Again, crickets from Kauffman.

In 1970, fans called the Royals' switchboard and complimented the field while watching a national telecast and asked what kind of artificial turf it was.

The switchboard operator told them it was grass.

However, Municipal Stadium was showing its age.

In 1972, I wrote a letter to the editor with problems the stadium had in its last season.

Knowing my continuous concerns on drainage were ignored, I said the clubhouse was filthy and needed some paint and that tin fell off the stadium.

I said Municipal Stadium is a grand old lady.

"Let's keep her smiling through 1972 so she can go out in style," I wrote. "I've given up on the drainage, but a little elbow grease and supervision can keep her in fashion."

In 1976, Municipal Stadium was demolished. Parts of the stadium were plowed under. It's now the site of many single-family homes.

When the Truman Sports Complex opened in the fall of 1972 for football and 1973 for baseball, the complex was spread over 60 acres with 5,000 trees.

In other words, our crew kept busy.

Kauffman also had my crew taking care of his mansion and cutting grass. We also had to send Harold Myers, a retired man the crew loved like a father, to the home of the CEO of Marion Laboratories – and take care of his place.

One day, Harold came back crying.

"You lied to me," he said before telling me they also made him wash the CEO's cars, clean the swimming pool and defrost the freezer.

When a story ran on the first page of the Kansas City Star outlining Ewing Kauffman's treatment of the workers, he told a writer, "If George Toma and his crew don't like what they're doing, they can get a job someplace else. I am paying him $10,000 a year."

Finally, when we complained to Kauffman's chauffeur and Mrs. Kauffman heard about the CEO, they stopped it right there.

Because both teams used Municipal Stadium, the Athletics/Royals and Chiefs agreed to split the costs for the groundskeepers and landscapers. If one of the teams was short-handed and the other needed help, they brought more help over.

So Chiefs owner Lamar Hunt paid us to take care of Kauffman's and the CEO's yards. And Mr. Hunt never knew because I never told him.

When Mrs. Kauffman got involved, the situation improved tremendously. She hired two high school students who she helped work their way through college. Her daughter Sue and son John also were outstanding.

Now, their daughter, Julia Irene, saw me talking to Reggie Jackson and told Royals executive Herk Robinson she wanted me fired. God bless Connie Leonard, the switchboard operator who answered, "Who the hell are you?"

However, I have to admit, Julia Irene did a good job helping Herk Robinson run the Royals. Still, few in the organization stood up to Kauffman.

Finally, I got myself an agent, Chuck Rubin, who represented golfer Tom Watson. Rubin made Herk feel so bad I got a better deal. Still didn't get paid much better, but I did get some benefits. I fought hard to earn respect for myself and my grounds crews.

On Sept. 5, 2023, Herk called. He had been with the Royals for 41 years in various capacities, including general manager.

Robinson shared that he wished he and upper management had treated my staff better. I think he realized those young men helped the Kansas City baseball teams look good. I appreciated him doing that because my guys really give it their best – and then some.

In 2022, Charlie Keegan with TV station KSHB came to a reunion that myself and a lot of grounds crew attended at the former site of Municipal Stadium on 22nd Street and Brooklyn Avenue. Roland brought along his World Series ring.

"They love George," Nelson said. "He was a little hard sometimes, and when he saw you slacking, he'd get on your ass. We joked later in life, he taught us something."

When I was inducted into the Kansas Sports Hall of Fame in October of 2022, I said, "If it wasn't for these people and their parents, there would be no George Toma today, and I say this worldwide."

5

Super Endorsements

"Put on whatever you want,
George. It's your field."

– NFL Commissioner Pete Rozelle in response
to George Toma's question of what kind
of logo he wanted at midfield for Super Bowl I

Working at Kansas City Municipal Stadium in the 1960s kept me busy because four professional teams shared the field:

The Kansas City Athletics from 1955 to 1967
The Kansas City Royals from 1969 to 1972
The Kansas City Chiefs from 1963 to 1971
The Kansas City Spurs from 1968 to 1970

The Spurs were members of the North American Soccer League. While the team had a short life in Kansas City, it was enough time to get a wonderful endorsement.

Pele and the Brazilian team Santos came to Kansas City in 1968 for a match against the Spurs. After the match, Pele told the media Municipal Stadium was the second-best field he played on. He called Wembley Stadium in London No. 1.

When Lamar Hunt moved the Kansas City Chiefs to Municipal Stadium, he treated me well so I wanted to give him a really nice field.

Because a football field is torn up by 22 players – and their 44 cleats – on the grass at the same time and the weather is cooler in the fall and winter, the way we planted grass had to be different than for baseball.

I knew what to do.

I had worked Pennsylvania football fields in Edwardsville as well as Artillery Park in Wilkes-Barre from 1942 to 1950. My uncle bought me a line marker, which I carried on my shoulder over the railroad tracks and the Susquehanna River bridge. I then took it to Meyers High School, where I earned $25 for lining the fields.

So what did we do?

We seeded from Aug. 15 to Sept. 1, mainly for baseball although football benefited. When football started, we seeded in the fall.

After the last baseball game – usually on a Sunday – we'd take a 4-foot-by-6-foot nail drag and plow the field while lowering the pitching mound and putting pre-germinated rye grass on the infield dirt.

By Friday, that grass grew so much we could cut it. By Saturday, we painted the lines. And by Sunday, teams played on it. After games, we'd sweep, mow, pin spike it and add more pre-germinated rye grass.

We also seeded in November so it would make grass grow for the next year.

Adding Color To Green

I often lay in bed at night thinking what we could do to make the field better. Often, I thought more about correcting something.

But one night, a creative idea came to mind.

For the Chiefs' first home game in Kansas City in 1963, I had a special surprise: painted end zones and an emblem at midfield.

In the old days, I created hand-made stencils when painting the field.

For the Chiefs' end zone, we put the paint in used two-gallon Hudson steel galvanized sprayers. Using 1-inch-by-2-inch lumber, I made my own stencils. We didn't have specialty equipment back then.

One frame was put in another frame three feet inside.

The background was painted gold with the Chiefs' name in red. We also inserted the AFL logo. The Chiefs' letters were 10 feet wide and 15 feet high.

By positioning the boards in different ways and at different angles, we could make the letters.

We also made line boards, like a trough, and those still are used today.

I think everyone loved the added color. I know Mr. Hunt did. In future games, he wanted the Chiefs' logo with the point of the arrow red and the tail yellow. Today the logo has a KC inside the arrowhead with black trim. An all-red CHIEFS is painted in all caps in the end zone.

In 2022, the Chiefs invited me to paint the arrowhead logo, and in 2023, they wanted me to show them how I painted the end zones for the 60-year anniversary.

Owners Butted Heads

My biggest problem was that Charles O. Finley and Lamar Hunt didn't get along. I think it started when Kansas City officials gave Hunt that $1 lease. Finley wanted the same deal but was turned down originally.

This led to several battles between Finley and the city that included a lawsuit. On Feb. 26, 1964, he was supposed to take part in a four-year signing ceremony. Instead, he sent his attorneys.

When Kansas City officials floated the idea of a domed stadium that would house both the Chiefs and the Athletics, Finley made it clear he didn't want to have to share a facility with Hunt. That led to the Truman Sports Complex idea where the teams would have their own stadiums and share the parking lot. However, shortly after Kansas City voters approved the sports complex, Finley left for Oakland following the 1967 season.

With plans to build a stadium but no team, powerful Missouri senator Stuart Symington threatened to revoke Major League Baseball's antitrust exemption, which led MLB officials to grant the city a new franchise – the Kansas City Royals.

Because the American League needed an even number of teams, the Seattle Pilots also were granted a franchise. They later became the Milwaukee Brewers.

And because the National League wanted the same number of teams as the American League, the Montreal Expos and San Diego Padres became expansion teams.

Basically, Charles O. Finley's move led to the creation of four new MLB teams.

That may have been his best baseball promotion of all.

Hunt's Promotions

Mr. Hunt had a lot of good ideas, such as creating a group of fans called the Wolfpack, whose members sat in 50 rows of bleachers.

He also helped me put up chairs behind the home plate area. When I wanted to put in aisles, he said, "No aisles. Do you know how much money you're taking away from me?"

Finding an opportunity to bring in more fans, Hunt added more seats when the city demolished the hillside and put in concrete flooring in the back of one of the end zones. There also were concession stands and bathrooms.

He then had a welder come in and put in a railing that fans could lean on. Standing-room only. Mr. Hunt said he got the idea when he went to a soccer match in England.

I also met Bill McNutt, one of Mr. Hunt's friends, who ran Collin Street Bakery, a large fruitcake bakery in Corsicana, Texas. For $1, Bill would send us a fruitcake every Christmas. He also helped me come up with the idea of painting logos on the field.

Bill died in 2006, but I still pay his family $1 to get these world-famous fruitcakes every holiday. Sweet deal.

Municipal Stadium seated about 34,000 fans, and they were packed for the Chiefs' games on Sundays. The city fell in love with the team.

When Kansas City scored a touchdown, Bob Johnson and sometimes Tony DiPardo, the band leader, would ride on Warpaint, a pinto horse who was the team's mascot.

In 1967, the Chiefs beat the Chicago Bears 66-24 in an exhibition game for their first win over an NFL team. Bears Hall of Fame linebacker Dick Butkus, who died in 2023, wasn't nearly as upset about the score as he was worried that we'd kill Warpaint after making him run from one end zone to the other after all those touchdowns.

Rave Reviews

NFL teams noticed what great shape the field was in. New York Jets coach Weeb Ewbank told his players on the

Saturday walk-throughs, "Work out on the sidelines. Stay off the field. That field is too beautiful to play on."

Chiefs executive Jack Steadman, who loaned me to the NFL, said, "I know we're not paying you enough and when you leave it will take three guys to replace you."

Famous last words.

Joe Foss, the AFL commissioner, also said some nice things. I respected that he was a Marine Corps veteran.

In November 1966, NFL Commissioner Pete Rozelle visited Municipal Stadium. Talk of a merger between the NFL and AFL started to heat up. When asked about the

At the request of Tex Schramm, I helped work the field for the Dallas Cowboys first Thanksgiving game on color TV.

difference between the two leagues, Rozelle said, "I don't see too much."

Then he added, "But I have never seen such a beautiful playing field. ... I've never seen a playing surface like the one here in Kansas City."

That hit the papers.

A day later, Tex Schramm, general manager of the Dallas Cowboys, asked to borrow me for a week to work the Cotton Bowl field for a Thanksgiving night game against the Cleveland Browns. Schramm told me he wanted the field to look in good shape because it would be the Cowboys' first nationally televised NFL game shown in color.

Less than six weeks later, Schramm, the NFL's most powerful GM – and close friends with Rozelle – had me do a doubleheader.

On Dec. 31, 1966 – the Georgia Bulldogs and Southern Methodist Mustangs met in the Cotton Bowl Classic.

The next day – Jan. 1, 1967 – the Dallas Cowboys played the Green Bay Packers for the NFL championship.

We had less than 24 hours to get the field in shape. We worked all night.

We also brought in a helicopter to blow the debris into the stands. The helicopter also dried the paint on the field.

Before Christmas, Rozelle approached me and gave me an appointment that would change my life.

Rozelle asked if I'd like to be head groundskeeper for the NFL-AFL championship game, later to be called the Super Bowl. And I had carte blanche.

After Mr. Rozelle gave his blessing on midfield, I came up with the idea to paint a gold crown on top of a football. NFL-AFL and 1967 were all written above the ball.

This was the only year this style was used at midfield.

For me, it would be Year 1 of 57.

Major League Baseball teams in St. Louis, Atlanta, Boston and Baltimore offered me jobs with increased pay, while the New York Yankees offered to double my salary as well as give me a playoff share.

Me with former NFL commissioner Pete Rozelle. Thanks to Rozelle's appointment, I became the head groundskeeper for the first NFL-AFL championship game.

But I decided to stay in Kansas City. City officials showed their appreciation. Over the years, I received a proclamation from Mayor Charles Wheeler in the 1970s and a resolution from Mayor Richard Berkley in 1985 after Super Bowl 19.

I became a member of the Kansas City Walk of Stars in 1996 and Jackson County officials recognized me with George Toma Day on April 14, 2019.

The Royals honored me by putting me in their Hall of Fame in 2012, the same year I was inducted into the Major League Baseball Groundskeepers Hall of Fame.

I've told many people that if it weren't for all the people who worked for the Royals as well as the sportswriters, I wouldn't be in the Hall of Fame. Any of them.

Maybe it was fate that I stayed in KC.

"We were the first team to have painted end zones and an emblem at midfield," Lamar Hunt said. "Pete (Rozelle) wanted the Super Bowl field to look like ours did.

"If Pete hadn't come to town, George may never have gone on to do the Super Bowls."

6

Superball, Super Bowl

"I have kiddingly called it the 'Super Bowl,' which obviously can be improved upon."

– Kansas City Chief owner Lamar Hunt in a July 25, 1966, letter to NFL Commissioner Pete Rozelle

In the more than 60 years I've known the Hunt family, I have three rings from the first three Super Bowl titles the Chiefs won. To my complete surprise, they presented the third one to me in October of 2023. I also was invited to the Super Bowl pregame festivities. Pretty amazing because I hadn't worked for the Chiefs for 35 years.

On June 4, 2023, I saw Lamar Hunt Jr. at the George P. Toma Wiffle Ball Field at the Hollow. He had brought senior citizens and schoolchildren for the day to watch and play wiffle ball.

I asked how his mother, Norma, was doing.

"Oh, she's great," Lamar Hunt Jr. said. "Thanks for asking."

A few hours later, I went home, turned on the television and saw that Norma Hunt had passed away. What a wonderful woman.

When the Kansas City Chiefs opened their 2023 season, they wore NKH patches on their jerseys to honor her.

Norma Hunt is part of Super Bowl history. She married Lamar Hunt, the Kansas Chiefs' original owner; she played a role in the naming of the NFL championship game; and she attended the first 57 Super Bowls. After neither of us attended Super Bowl LVIII in 2024, there aren't many left who have been to every game.

You can just about count them on one hand now.

I remember the first Super Bowl as well as the 57th.

In the days leading up to the Chiefs' Super Bowl I contest against the Green Bay Packers, Mr. Hunt asked me to drive with him to pick up Norma at the airport. I took a quick shower, then joined him in the lobby of the Sheraton.

When we went to the parking lot, the car was gone. Coach Hank Stram took it, something he did all the time.

After trying to find someone with a car, we finally rented one for a few hours from a man who worked in the Sheraton's kitchen.

The beat-up station wagon we rented was on its last wheels. To make matters worse, we got lost and ended up in Watts. The beat-up car may have been a blessing in disguise there. Just 17 months earlier, riots took place in the Watts neighborhood and the surrounding areas of Los Angeles in August 1965. Finally, we made it to the airport. When Norma saw us, she sat down and started laughing. She never lost the common touch. Neither did her husband, who listed his phone number in the Kansas City phone book.

Superball

I remember Norma regularly sitting with the rowdy Wolfpack in the bleachers.

In 1966, she bought her children Zectron Superballs, introduced by Wham-O. They were considered the bounciest balls ever made.

When Lamar Hunt saw his children playing with the balls, he started thinking, "Superball, Super Bowl."

Me with Norma Hunt, wife of former Kansas City Chiefs owner Lamar Hunt at Super Bowl 50.

However, he wasn't convinced that this should be the name of the NFL's championship game. Neither was NFL Commissioner Pete Rozelle. Even fellow NFL owners chuckled when hearing it.

"If possible, I believe we should 'coin a phrase' for the Championship Game," Hunt wrote, according to Michael MacCambridge's book America's Game. "I have kiddingly called it the 'Super Bowl,' which obviously can be improved upon."

Rozelle and Hunt settled on the "AFL-NFL Championship Game" for the first couple of years.

Manicuring the field for the first title game in Los Angeles was a pretty normal procedure. I arrived five days early and worked with a small screw of men and a man named Bob Williams. They were all hard workers.

They had this sprayer they took everywhere. I had a 3-foot-by-4-foot trunk with all the equipment I needed. I still have that trunk in my basement.

We cut the field, swept it, groomed it, watered it with Hudson metal garden sprayers and painted the lines and the logos. Today, we start field preparations weeks in advance. About 30 men and two 45-foot tractor trailers full of equipment are involved.

For the first 27 Super Bowls, we spent between $500 and $1,000. Now, I believe the cost had increased to an estimated $700,000 to $800,000 for the field and maintenance.

Has it been better? I'll hold off on my opinion on that for now.

For the first championship game, some media originally named it "The World Series of Football." However, others followed Mr. Hunt's lead and called it the Super Bowl. If you watch NFL Films in its 30-minute highlight montage of the first title game, producers called it Super Bowl I.

Finally, by Super Bowl III, the name stuck.

Some wondered what kind of future the Super Bowl had when the first game had about 30,000 empty seats. However, we later found out that more than 65 million people had watched the game. Both CBS and NBC televised it. I thought the younger generation would be interested in the game.

The Orange Bowl in Miami played host to the next two Super Bowls.

When we arrived for Super Bowl II, the Green Bay Packers vs. the Oakland Raiders, the field was in bad shape. At that

Whether I was overseeing Super Bowls or back in Kansas City, I was always working and I loved it. There was always something that needed to be done.

time, the NFL had a runner-up game the week before the Super Bowl, and that year it was played in the rain.

When we arrived on Monday, there was a clarinet embedded near the center of the field.

Because we only had a week, Dr. James Watson and I came up with a recipe to get the grass to grow quicker.

It's called pre-germination. We took 100 pounds of rye grass seeds and placed them in 55-gallon drums.

On Day 1, the seeds were soaked for eight hours in water containing Bov-A-Mura – liquid cow manure – and Aqua-Zorb, a wetting agent. This solution is removed and the barrels are refilled with fresh water every eight hours.

Within four days, the seeds sprouted. We then mixed it with equal amounts of Milorganite fertilizer or calcined clay in a cement mixer. Calcined clay really soaks up the water.

As NFL special events director Jim Steeg will attest, it's a smell you just don't forget unless you drive past Midwest

Pictures of me through the years with Len Dawson, Kansas City's quarterback in Super Bowl I and Super Bowl III. He was a real gentleman.

farms in the middle of the summer.

During this process, we paid more attention to the temperature of the seed in the barrel and how long it sat in the water. The seeds needed air and moisture and had to stay within a certain temperature range.

After aerifying the field lightly, we applied the seeds to the soil with pin spikers.

By Friday, we could cut the grass, and Saturday we could paint it. Gametime was Sunday.

It's the same process we used until Super Bowl XXVII in 1993.

Sometimes, there's only so much you can do.

Super Bowl IV in 1970 had a bare field in New Orleans. The end zone had hardly any grass. During the week, the weather was freezing. There was a big storm the night before the game, and the restrooms froze.

What I did during the week was put down wood chips, scatter sawdust and paint the field green. There were wet spots, but the players didn't complain because they still had good footing.

I remember Otis Taylor running by me after catching a 46-yard pass from Len Dawson to seal the Chiefs' 23-7 victory over the Minnesota Vikings.

For two years in a row, AFL teams had won against their NFL foes, and the merger between the leagues showed the title game wouldn't be as one-sided as some thought. In fact, after Green Bay's first two Super Bowl wins, the AFL/AFC teams would win eight of the next nine contests.

Little did we know it would be 50 years before Kansas City would return to the Big Game.

But I kept returning year after year.

This letter from the commissioner shows what the NFL thought of my work:

PETE ROZELLE
410 Park Avenue
New York

Feb. 6, 1978

Dear George,

The enclosed column from a Tampa area paper pleased me greatly because I like you to know that your work is noticed and greatly appreciated by others in the league office.

But, of course, we must be your #1 fans! The Super Bowl was just magnificent and I heard so many compliments about it from those at the game, I only wish you could have heard them, too. And certainly, no Pro Bowl field ever looked better.

Thank you for always giving something extra and achieving an outstanding result whether under controlled conditions of a domed stadium or while contending with adverse weather conditions outside.

Incidentally, this is my version of a handwritten letter – a throwback to my old days as a P.R. man. Best wishes always.

Regards,

Pete

7

Carpet vs. Sod

"I don't know. I never smoked the fake stuff."

– Former major league pitcher Bill Lee on whether he preferred natural grass or artificial turf.

When Major League Baseball granted Houston an expansion franchise in 1960, one of the reasons was that county officials promised to build the first all-enclosed, air-conditioned stadium in the world.

Since it became apparent early that grass couldn't grow in the indoor facility, synthetic grass needed to be developed. Houston officials renamed their team the Astros. They called the stadium The Astrodome and the "grass" was called AstroTurf.

The Astros were named after astronauts because Houston is home to Mission Control Center at NASA's Johnson Space Center, but that's another story.

Soon, other professional teams went to artificial turf. From 1971 to 1982, the Super Bowl was played on that surface eight times.

Even though I personally was a lot stiffer after walking a

day on artificial turf than on natural grass, my feelings on the two surfaces are the same:

It's not the surface but the person who takes care of the surface.

People used to send me requests for boxes of dirt so they could copy the formula and put them on their fields. While the right mix is important, what makes the difference is the person or crew who takes care of the dirt.

If a team puts in grass and you don't maintain it, it's going to be bad.

And if a team puts in artificial turf and you don't maintain it, it's going to be bad. Tobacco juice (ammonia), bubble gum (gum freeze and scrape) and shoe stains (ammonia) are some of the stuff that needs to be cleaned. Artificial turf doesn't need fertilizers, but you have to clean the turf. You don't have to cut it, but you do have to sweep it.

I remember telling Del Black of Ingram's Magazine how I had to train guys where to spit.

At the end of the day, it's about the man – or woman.

While it took five years for the Astrodome to be built, Houston fans roasted in Colt Stadium, known as "The Sizzler" or "The Skillet." Players often lost between 10 and 12 pounds in sweat per game. Sort of like Kansas City in July and August.

Even though the Astrodome started being called "The Eighth Wonder of the World," the debut season in 1965 was an embarrassment when the grass turned brown and had to be painted green.

Monsanto came up with ChemGrass, a short-fiber, dense nylon carpet that was installed over a compacted soil base in the stadium. In other words, artificial turf.

Let George Do It

When the Kansas City Chiefs and Kansas City Royals moved to the Truman Sports Complex in 1972 and 1973, they had their own venues. However, they joined stadiums and ballparks around the country using artificial turf.

Part of the reason turned out to be expenses as well as wear-and-tear on grass. Many of the professional, cookie-cutter facilities were used for both football and baseball. Even the Orange Bowl, a football-only stadium, went to poly turf after it had 34 games played on it in 1968 between high school, college and the pros.

By 1973, I had started to gain some popularity in Kansas City, and the thought of fans' favorite groundskeeper overseeing artificial turf fields didn't sit well. CBS' Heywood Hale Broun compared me transitioning to maintaining artificial turf fields at the Truman Sports Complex to "a concert violinist doomed to run a discotheque."

Pretty soon, they made bumper stickers and had aerial banners flown that said, "Let George Do It."

I just took orders. I'm a grass man, what do I know about turf? But 3M's first foray into sports turf turned into an embarrassment. When they made me do a punch list of Royals Stadium, I raised a stink.

"There are not enough coffee tables in Kansas City to hide all the bad spots," I said.

When Royals management insisted I do the assessment, I didn't hold back. I got the great young men from Lincoln Preparatory Academy and Central High to assist, walking the field inch-by-inch and putting yellow tape on any bad spot.

More than 500 tape marks later, we showed how bad the field was. 3M architects, representatives and engineers mockingly laughed at us, but a few months later, they had to replace that field on their own dime.

3M left behind a big roll of turf for patching. Slowly but surely, the roll of turf got smaller and smaller. I don't know this for sure, but my theory is ballplayers, then other employees, cut off pieces. Probably laid them down on their porches or made makeshift batting cages at home or used them for putting or hitting golf balls.

Royals general manager Herk Robinson demanded to know what happened, but we all feigned innocence.

We were like Sergeant Schultz in Hogan's Heroes. We knew nothing.

This time, we had the last laugh.

Messy, Messy People

I don't know who caused me the most problems – umpires or San Diego Chargers coach Tommy Prothro.

Umpires spit almost as much as the players. The first- and third-base umpires would stand by the lines and spit all nine innings. Left a big brown spot at the end of the game. But we got along great. They were some of my best friends.

George Brett, one of my all-time favorites, was one of the few players to take extra time, walk over and spit on the dirt. Great, thoughtful, generous guy. He wrote the foreword in my first book, *Nitty Gritty Dirt Man* and he was

Me with my dear friend George Brett, a Kansas City Royals legend who was inducted into the Baseball Hall of Fame in 1999 on the first ballot.

my presenter when I was inducted into the Royals Hall of Fame. He had over 3,000 career hits and a lifetime batting average of .305.

A chain smoker, Prothro left big black marks on Arrowhead Stadium's field with more than 30 cigarette butts during a game. I told Tom Marshall of the Kansas City Star that I chewed his ass out from the 20-yard line to midfield, and he apologized.

Football players also made black marks when their plastic or rubber spikes slid against the turf. Heat would fuse the artificial grass fibers together.

By taking ammonia solution along with steel brushes and a paint brush comb with sharp needles we bought in a hardware store, we kept the field looking green.

Despite Herk Robinson's warnings that we were going to wear out the field by sweeping and washing it, we kept cleaning. The field lasted 13 years.

The work we did on Royals Stadium and Arrowhead Stadium once again got the NFL's attention.

Cincinnati Bengals owner Paul Brown wanted Riverfront Stadium to look like Arrowhead. He told his groundskeeper, Darian Daily, and I worked with him. He did a fine job until dying after suffering a medical emergency in 2016.

Cincinnati now has a new field – Paycor Stadium – and Brown's son Mike also wants it to look as good as Arrowhead.

The NFL also had me go to Chicago and Philadelphia after players got knee injuries.

Research back then showed that artificial turf, which isn't as giving as grass, led to more ankle, foot, knee, hip and shoulder injuries. Colorado Buffaloes coach Deion Sanders, more than 15 years after his NFL career ended, had two toes amputated as a result of injuries from his playing days. Many of you may be familiar with the term turf toe.

My biggest concern was keeping the artificial turf clean. If you don't keep it clean, it can get slippery. And if you don't keep it clean, players could get nasty infections when their elbows, arms, fingers and knees scrape against the turf.

Fixing poly turf at the Orange Bowl for Super Bowl V in 1971 wasn't difficult. The biggest problem was getting removable paint. If it was aluminum paint, we also had to use an ammonia solution to remove it.

We washed the end zones and logos, and it worked.

Super Sod

My good friend Eddie Woerner is like me.

We never attended a day of college. Our education came by way of listening, reading and learning by trial and error.

Today, we can teach college students, agronomists and those with a master's degree in turf management a thing or two.

In fact, we have.

I grew grass on artificial turf, which helped FIFA award the World Cup to the United States in 1994.

On Aug. 28, 1999, we gave the New Orleans Superdome an aroma it never had before – fresh-cut grass.

The Green Bay Packers said they'd only play the New Orleans Saints in an exhibition game if they inserted grass on the synthetic playing field.

Eddie Woerner had been experimenting with planting grass on plastic on his farm in Elberta, Ala. He was ahead of everybody. Using a grass called STN 2000, he could get it to grow laterally and wrap around other grasses like a python.

While growing samples of a rugged grass called seashore paspalum, Woerner and his staff noticed the compressed root system had twisted and weaved into a solid mass, making the grass even more durable and sturdy. Elberta high school football players gave the turf its first test.

On the Tuesday before the Saints-Packers game, 33 semis arrived and delivered 90,000 square feet of rolled-up turf grown by Southern Turf Nurseries, Eddie Woerner's farm.

"This is a new day for us," Woerner told the New Orleans Times-Picayune. "We have not only taken our natural grass and created a rug, but we also have designed the equipment for installation and removal in record time. We have built a natural-grass system that provides an excellent alternative as a tough-playing surface."

We put plastic sheeting down, then came the STN 2000. Eddie had sod cut 7 feet wide and 40 feet long so we could fit it on a truck. A machine laid it.

On Thursday, Saints coach Mike Ditka and his players gave positive reviews. After watching his players cut and run on the field, Ditka said, "It'll work." He even did a quick down-and-out. "Wonderful," he said.

I said it was the finest sod I had seen in 59 years.

"George, sweep it up and let's play a doubleheader," Ditka said.

Quarterback Billy Joe Hobert said, "I like the feel."

Wide receiver Andre Hastings added, "Love it. We should use it for all of our games."

Mike Ditka, left, me and groundskeeper Ken Mrock in Berlin.

I wanted to get industrial-strength fans to dry the paint on the field, but when that wasn't available, I had an idea.

Working with WWL 870-AM, Bob DelGiorno asked listeners to bring their airboats to the Superdome, according to the Times-Picayune.

Wayne Ponthieux, who had four airboats in his swamp tour business, obliged.

With their 450-horsepower engines, the airboats created gale-force winds on the grass. Two boats were on one sideline, one boat was on the other sideline, and a fourth boat was behind the end zone.

We then put up a sign no Superdome employees thought they'd ever see: KEEP OFF THE GRASS. Long-time Times-Picayune writer Peter Finney wrote about it.

To top it all off, two cows from the Louisiana Dairy Farms Association grazed on the field. They provided natural fertilizer. The field was rolled on the turf in 23 hours and rolled off in 12.

Green Bay quarterback Brett Favre called it fast grass. Teammate LeRoy Butler told USA Today that he hoped other NFL operators took notice. "I think every domed team should try this by next year," he said.

The Packers are one of the few NFL teams to use a combination of grass and synthetic turf on their field.

"Can you believe that little old me, a guy who's been in the sports grass business for all of five years, got to do this?" Woerner said. "Unbelievable."

The Debate Continues

It seems every few years, there's an exposé written on which is better – carpet or sod.

The quality of artificial turf has improved a lot the last few years, a big reason 17 of the 32 NFL teams have it.

The best artificial turf crew is at SoFi Stadium, home to the Los Angeles Rams and Chargers. We didn't even need a crew for Super Bowl LVI in 2022, the field was so spotless. They kept it clean all the way to game time.

Standing next to a larger-than-life size cut out of me at the George P. Toma Wiffle Ball Field.

The Houston grounds crew's work on NRG Stadium puts it on par with Sofi Stadium. Kudos Kevin Hansen.

However, many studies have shown the majority of NFL players don't like artificial turf.

Twenty-five out of 30 ballparks in Major League Baseball have grass fields, including the Kansas City Royals, who switched in 1995. I threw out the first pitch for that first game on the new grass field while wearing a tuxedo. The

Royals drove me out in a 1957 Cadillac Convertible because that's the year I arrived.

I think grass fields are great for the senses.

I enjoy the sound of a field being mowed.

When fans enter the stadium, they see the beautifully manicured field with intricate mowing patterns.

Ballplayers can smell the cut grass or pick up a blade and taste it.

When I looked over a field after my crew and I prepared it, grass or turf, I always felt a sense of pride as we gave it our best – and then some.

We felt like it was the best surface the players ever had.

8

The Super Bowl Evolves

"It was a football game. Now it's a monster.
Jim put the right people in place and made it what it is."

– Don Renzulli, formerly the NFL's
senior director of events, on Jim Steeg

In the late 1970s and early 1980s, Super Bowl interest took off. According to The Sports Business Journal's Terry Lefton, from the 1980 season to the 2005 season:

The domestic TV audience grew from 68.2 million to 90.7 million.

The cost of a 30-second ad in the game skyrocketed from $275,000 to $2.5 million.

Super Bowl revenue reportedly had increased from $5 million to $250 million.

The face value of a ticket increased from $30 to $600.

While NFL Commissioner Pete Rozelle deservedly receives a lot of credit for building the Super Bowl, a hire he made in January 1979 played a huge role in the Big Game prospering.

His name? Jim Steeg, who became the NFL's special events

director. Jim worked for the Miami Dolphins, and Rozelle hired him just before other NFL teams could pry him away.

I couldn't agree more with Don Renzulli's comment. During Jim's leadership, we hardly had any problems from Super Bowl XIV in 1980 to Super Bowl XXXIX in 2005. When he left, Rozelle trusted Jim so much, he also had him run the NFL draft, which has turned into a television bonanza and moved to bigger and bigger venues besides New York City.

It was in Kansas City in 2023.

Jim increased revenue because he came up with ideas such as logos on the pylons, sponsors' names on nets behind the goalposts, celebrity anthems and halftime concerts by pop stars.

He also spearheaded Super Bowl merchandise in area hotels, corporate hospitality villages, the NFL Experience for fans and the Super Bowl winner presentation moving from the locker room to the field where confetti dropped.

"When you start getting covered by "The National Enquirer" about the selection of the national anthem singer, you know you've hit a different strata," Jim told Michael Mayo of the Sun-Sentinel in 1995.

But the game remained No. 1.

Halftime show rehearsals were in the parking lot in the days leading up the game, and rehearsals on the field were kept to three hours.

Even Michael Jackson's complicated show at the Rose Bowl in 1993 didn't go past 180 minutes.

He and his production crew also had to practice in a tent. When casters were used for a stage and they stuck onto the field, we had to use a forklift to get the stage back up. Steeg tried to help us with the field by putting balloon tires under the stage.

This letter from Steeg to Kansas City Chiefs executive Jack Steadman explained how the NFL asked for my services:

Oct. 6, 1980

Mr. Jack Steadman, President
KANSAS CITY CHIEFS
One Arrowhead Drive
Kansas City, Missouri 64129

Dear Jack:

We would like once again to have the incomparable George Toma as our Super Bowl groundskeeper and request your permission to "borrow" him starting December 31, 1980 so he can begin preparations for the January 25 game.

Despite this year's game being indoors on artificial turf, we have added problems with the field as there are events on the Superdome's floor starting January 1 till January 19. It is going to be tight getting everything done prior to the teams' arrivals.

We would like to "borrow" George for the Pro Bowl again this year. As you know, the game will be in Honolulu on February 1.

As you know, George is a member of the Super 14 club – that distinguished group that has been part of either the working or coverage force for each of the previous games. With your permission, we'd like to make that XV.

Sincerely,

JAMES H. STEEG
Director of Special Events

As field supervisors, I (1967-1995) and son Chip (1996-2000) regularly visited sod farms as well as Super Bowl sites and checked on practice and game fields. We also communicated with Jim regularly from August until we arrived at the Super Bowl site. As the letter mentioned, we came out early for the Super Bowl. Sometimes we'd go before Christmas; sometimes we'd go around Thanksgiving, if a college football team also played on the field.

And just to be safe, we always went to the Big Game with two tarps when we were outdoors. We always had to be prepared for rain.

The groundskeeping staff Chip and I put together worked as a team. Everyone knew his or her role, and there were no egos. After the Super Bowls, Jim, Chip, the staff and I reviewed how the event went – both the practice and game fields – to see what improvements could be made in the future.

Chip shared a typical daily conversation with Jim leading up the Big Game:

Jim Steeg and I made a great team.

"He'd always ask, 'How are the practice fields looking?' I'd say, 'They're good. I have two guys out there, and everything is going well. I talked with the coach, and he also had an assistant or host for anything needed.'

"He'd then say, 'Were you guys happy today? Are you OK?' Then he'd ask, 'Do you want to make any changes tomorrow?'"

Employee No. 46

Terry Lefton wrote that Jim became the NFL's 46th employee. The league now has approximately 3,600 employees under its umbrella. The number has tripled since Roger Goodell became commissioner in 2006. There also are dozens of employees who have been given the title of vice president.

Jim, Don Renzulli and Billy Granholm did everything from making sure there were enough hangers in the players' locker rooms to getting the scoreboard lights working to ensuring all details were ironed out when the president of the United States attended the game. When the halftime show needed bigger celebrities, Jim brought in The Rolling Stones, Paul McCartney, Bruce Springsteen and The Who.

He even got Garth Brooks to return to sing the national anthem at Super Bowl XXVII in 1993 after he got upset when a music video of his had not run on NBC before the game.

Lefton wrote that Jim's mastery of detail is perhaps best exemplified by Super Bowl XXX in 1996, played in Tempe, Ariz. Halftime show performer Diana Ross planned to exit Sun Devil Stadium in a helicopter that would land on the stage. Jim told the governor of Arizona, the Arizona State University president and NFL President and COO Neil Austrian that if any of the cups on the sidelines blew away, the helicopter exit was off. However, he knew the helicopter departure would work because he had done his own rehearsal beforehand.

I remember Ross' rehearsals lasted so long Eddie Mangan chased her and her crew off the field.

In later years, the halftime shows became more extravagant. There were 88 pianos on the field one year, then 100 motorcycles, then 42-ton stages, then 4,000 people rehearsing on the field.

As the NFL's championship game has evolved, the focus has shifted from the game to the halftime show. And that has created major issues with the fields.

With all these performers on the field, I had to implement a rule: When they came on the field, they could only do so in socks. My crew also wore socks on the field.

I told people that grass grew by the inch but it was killed by the feet.

Field Shift

Between Super Bowl V and Super Bowl XL in 2006, a total of 16 league championship games were played on artificial turf. Of those 16 championship games, 11 were played in domed stadiums in Atlanta, New Orleans, Detroit and Minneapolis.

However, the Super Bowl shifted to having more games played on grass.

A few reasons:

Stadiums like the Los Angeles Memorial Coliseum, Rose Bowl, Tampa Stadium, Stanford Stadium, Jack Murphy/ Qualcomm Stadium, Joe Robbie Stadium, Sun Devil Stadium and Alltel Stadium in Jacksonville kept grass fields.

The Orange Bowl returned to a grass field before it hosted Super Bowl XIII in 1979.

Reliant Stadium officials, helped by a retractable roof, were able to use a grass surface when they held Super Bowl XXXVIII in 2004. This led to grass fields at University of Phoenix Stadium and Allegiant Stadium, which hosted the Super Bowl LVIII in Las Vegas in 2024.

The Rose Bowl hosted the Super Bowl five times. While Chip and I surrounded ourselves with a good grounds crew, Chip said Jim surrounded himself with good people such as Billy Granholm and Joe Rhein. Jim wanted to be kept informed, but he had confidence people would get the job done.

"It reminded me of what my brother Rick told me," Chip said. "He was a tank commander in Desert Storm. "He always told me, 'We always got good inspections and good achievement certifications because I surrounded myself with good staff sergeants. It was my decision what we'd do in the end, but I listened to all those sergeants because they knew what was going on with the troops."

Chip added that Steeg wasn't all business.

"When we went to Europe, we'd take baseballs, bats, footballs," he said. "Then we'd play a baseball, football or basketball game to get away from work."

Jim also cared about those who he worked with.

In 1981, Chip's car hydroplaned during a rainy day and he was involved in a nasty car accident, which broke his neck. For almost 20 years, Chip constantly dealt with a lot of aches, but he started relying on pain killers too much.

Led by Jim Steeg, we did an intervention in 2000. We met him at his office and took him to the Menninger Foundation, a renowned treatment facility in Kansas. The NFL stepped in and covered all the costs.

Chip was smart to seek treatment for his addiction. Overdosing on prescription drugs continues to be a problem in the United States. More than 16,000 people die every year from overdosing on prescription opioids, according to the National Institute on Drug Abuse.

Between 1977 and 1993 (one was awarded because Arizona officials didn't acknowledge Martin Luther King Jr. Day), the Rose Bowl hosted five Super Bowls.

The main reason that ended was because the host Los Angeles Rams moved to St. Louis in 1995. The NFL also wanted to have its teams receive Super Bowls so they could complete stadium projects.

I loved being at and working at the Rose Bowl.

Rich Gonzales and the guys were outstanding, always a good crew.

Later I visited with Will Schnell, one of the best groundskeepers, at the Rose Bowl. While I got my start in

Wilkes-Barre, Will got his in Harrisburg, Pennsylvania, on City Island.

When we returned to the Rose Bowl for Super Bowl XXI in 1987, we had perfect conditions. Later, New York Giants coach Bill Parcells and Denver Broncos coach Dan Reeves called it "Astrograss."

Dry As A Beach

Like Garo Yepremian's crazy pass in Super Bowl VII in 1973 or Jackie Smith's drop in Super Bowl XIII in 1979, we had a few embarrassing moments.

The biggest problem we had came in Super Bowl XXIII.

We had Joe Robbie Stadium near Miami looking exactly how we wanted. The only thing that concerned us was not to turn on a pump that would dry the field.

It started to rain, so the tarp went on the field.

Just a couple of hours before kickoff, when I told Scott Martin to cut the grass, he said there was a funny sound. I thought it was the mower, but instead the pump was on.

By that time there was little we could do.

The field was as dry as a beach. It also wreaked havoc on the NFL's midfield logo. And I hate to say it, but it may have played a role in one of the worst injuries in the league's history.

On the 14th play of the game, Cincinnati Bengals defensive tackle Tim Krumrie, one of the toughest players in the NFL, suffered a broken leg while trying to tackle Roger Craig. When his cleats caught in the turf, his left leg graphically flopped around.

Krumrie had four breaks in his lower left leg: two in the tibia, one in the fibula and one in his ankle. He ended up with a compound, segmented fracture.

The guy showed his toughness by staying in the locker room until halftime. He then left because he didn't want his teammates to see him. He took a medevac helicopter to the hospital.

Just weeks later, Krumrie pushed a snowblower through

the Wisconsin slush in the winter of 1989 after surgeons implanted a 15-inch stabilizing nail inside his tibia. He returned to training camp the following fall.

The NFL did an investigation of what caused Krumrie's injury but found nothing.

I'm Going To Jail

Super Bowl XXV in Tampa, Florida, had to be the most emotional of all the games.

From a security standpoint, it also was the most intense.

1991. The Gulf War. Desert Storm. My son Rick in the heat of it all as a tank commander. Black Hawk helicopters flying over the stadium. Stars & Stripes. No electronic devices or cameras allowed. Metal detectors. Sharpshooters with rifles above the press box. Close to 500 federal, state and local law-enforcement officers from 22 agencies deployed around the stadium. Whitney Houston's national anthem. Tears in the eyes of many, mine included.

And to think I really felt I was going to miss the game. I thought the police were going to arrest me and put me in the hoosegow.

Breaking and entering. Destruction of university property. Stealing. Erratic driving. Vehicular damage.

Here's the story.

After Super Bowl XXIII, when the field turned into a beach and wiped out the midfield logo, I said to myself: "Nothing is going to hurt the NFL emblem again."

I have so much respect for the NFL logo that I've told friends and family I want it placed over my heart when I die. In 2013, that almost happened when I had aortic valve replacement and my chest popped open because the pain medications drove me crazy. I called Jim Steeg, and he proceeded to buy a blue blazer with the NFL shield on the crest along with a size 36 shirt.

Thank goodness that remained in a storage room.

So, here we are, Super Bowl XXV. As we had done so many times for this title game, we had pre-germinated Tampa

Stadium with rye seed. It looked beautiful.

However, with both teams practicing on Saturday along with longer halftime rehearsals – understandably, the NFL wanted a patriotic theme with more military presence – midfield wore out in a couple of places.

At 6 p.m. Saturday night – about 24 hours before kickoff – I looked at this beaten-down field and told our crew of 30, "We're going to resod."

Jim quickly said, "What the hell? You want to do what? It can't be done."

But I said, "Don't worry. I'm gonna do it." Jim trusted me. My 25 years of service to the Super Bowl earned me some trust.

Like Bill Parcells, I laid out my game plan:

Some of the crew would take out 1,000 square feet of sod in the middle of the field, the Super Bowl game field, while the rest of the crew went to get new sod.

Other crew members would bring their trucks and cars where we picked up new sod.

Destination? The University of Tampa soccer field.

We get to the field, and the gate is closed. Now I'm feeling like Gen. Patton.

"Ram the damn thing," I said. We broke the gate open.

The sod looked beautiful.

Now, we were respectful. Instead of taking the sod from the playing field, we took 12-inch squares – about 2½ inches thick – around the fence line until we got our 1,000 square feet.

We filled up the trucks and car trunks, just like if you went to a nursery to get strips to patch your lawn.

Wayne Ward, who ran the show in Tampa, was a helluva worker. He could do anything and everything. He stood out when we worked the Super Bowls. I enjoyed working with him and the Dolphins' Spud Williams.

By 3 a.m., we had the sod laid, tamped down and painted. I then said to Jim and facility manager Rick Nafe, "Now, I'm ready to go to jail."

The NFL avoided that by writing the University of Tampa a nice check.

The field held up well, and the Giants really liked it as they controlled the ball for two-thirds of the game. Still, they had to hold their breaths until Buffalo Bills kicker Scott Norwood missed a field goal in the final seconds.

The 20-19 Giants victory remains the closest game in Super Bowl history.

At Super Bowl LV in Tampa, the media had us re-enact our escapades.

While exhausted, I had incredible satisfaction from the turnaround we did on that field with little time to spare. As with our men in Iraq, it shows what can be done when there's a coordinated effort and everyone is working in unison.

Best news of all – Rick came home a year later.

And I never had to use my get-out-of-jail card.

Extra Time Spent In Jacksonville

When Jacksonville played host to Super Bowl XXXIX in 2005, the city lacked in two crucial areas: hotel rooms and practice fields.

Cruise ships became the answer for the first problem. Using a college and high school field answered the second.

Starting six months before the Super Bowl, we built practice fields at the University of North Florida and Bartram Trail High School. I had been recovering from prostate cancer, but at 75, I felt pretty good. Like my good friend George Brett said after his hemorrhoids, "All my problems are behind me."

I told Mark Long of The Associated Press we planted Bermuda while including established sod, which was something new.

We also used Eddie Woerner's sod for both practice fields.

We used Princess 77 from the Pennington Company and Jennings Turf Farm in Georgia on the main field.

We had a couple of issues at the high school field, one which was overblown.

Snakes came up through the drains because it was next to a swamp. And the New England Patriots complained about the field being slippery.

Patriots coach Bill Belichick made a stink publicly and said his players had to change their cleats. Truth was, Belichick had a walk-through and no player had cleats on but it still turned into a full-time practice. Quarterback Tom Brady shared that with Jim Steeg.

In a newspaper story, Brady said he had to change cleats three times. But when I asked him about it, Brady apologized to Jim and I and told the crew he was sorry.

While I'm looking through a small opening where the gate comes together, a security officer huffed and asked me what I wanted.

Ticked off at Belichick's comments, I said, "The Boston Bruins are on strike, and they sent down their Zamboni; I wanted to know how much time was left in practice so I could bring the Zamboni out and run it over the field if it's that slippery."

That got the security officer upset.

At the same time, students, upset that Belichick criticized their locker room as well as the field, started protesting. One sign said, "Belichick, Go Home."

Patriots owner Robert Kraft had to go over to the students and apologize. When Kraft came over to Saturday's walk-through at Jacksonville's stadium, he was ahead of the security officer I had a scrap with.

When Kraft saw me, he came over, gave me a big hug and put his arm around me. As I wrapped my arms around Kraft, I took my middle finger, lifted it up and gave the security officer a salute.

The security guard never bothered me again.

Belichick never said a word to me.

Winds Of Change

With Jim Steeg leaving after the 2004 season, it was the end of an era.

New commissioner, new Super Bowl administrator, new field supervisor.

The winds of change stirred in the air.

Storm clouds soon followed.

9

Nicknames, Friends, Honors

"In the middle of the field was this little man
in a white coat. I asked St. Peter, 'Who is the guy
in the white coat?' He looked up, kind of laughed
and said, 'Oh that's God. He thinks he's George Toma.' "

– Baseball owner Charles Finley sharing a dream he had

I've had a few nicknames in my day.

Nitty Gritty Dirt Man was the title of a book Alan Goforth wrote on me that was published in 2004.

Sultan of Sod.
God of Sod.
Michelangelo of Grass.
Turf Magician.
Diamond Cutter.
Sod Surgeon.
The Sodfather.

Sportswriters and columnists also got creative:

Phil Gianficaro: Listening to George Toma ramble on

about groundskeeping is like listening to Itzhak Perlman talk about the violin.

Dan Barreiro: George Toma is to groundskeeping what Mick Jagger is to rock n' roll.

Jeffrey Flanagan: You get the impression George Toma could grow grass in outer space.

Jim Torbik: George Paul Toma denies the rumor that he manicured the Colosseum surface in Rome when the lions and Christians squared off.

Even executives and one manager got into the act:

Owner Bill Veeck: He called me "a magical man."

Chiefs executive Jack Steadman: "He's absolutely the best in the business."

Former Chiefs general manager Jim Schaaf to the Kansas City Star's Bob Gretz: "Nobody alive can carry George's shovel."

NFL director of events Jim Steeg to Susan Gill: "George could grow grass on a pool table. I trust him with my life. His knowledge and conscientiousness are beyond belief."

Hall of Fame manager Billy Martin to writer John Garrity: "George Toma is the master."

Hell, I once had a service dog named after me.

And even Kansas City Royals owner Ewing Kauffman, who I had my moments with, wrote me a nice letter:

Mr. George Toma
Kansas City Royals Baseball Club
P.O. Box 1969
Kansas City, MO 64141

Dear George:

While listening to you on the pre-game radio broadcast Sunday, I was impressed again by your dedication and loyalty to the Royals. Throughout the year it has always pleased me tremendously when other knowledgeable baseball people in my suite view our beautiful stadium and comment upon its cleanliness. Their conversation usually ends with, "It is not only the most beautiful stadium but the most immaculate."

George, my personal thanks to you and your excellent crew for the fine job you do every day.

Sincerely,

Ewing M. Kauffman
EMK/sdc
Cc: Herk Robinson

In The Sporting News' 1982 Pro Football Yearbook, Oakland Athletics owner Charlie Finley shared a dream he had: "I died and went to heaven where St. Peter greeted me at the pearly gates. He read my card and said, 'So you like sports. I'm sure you'll want to see our stadium. It seats 500,000.'

"We went to see the stadium and it was a beautiful place with solid gold seats rimmed in platinum and studded with 50-carat diamonds. The field was immaculate, without a blade of grass out of place.

"In the middle of the field was this little man in a white coat. This guy was running around doing everything in sight, making grass grow here and cutting it there.

"I asked St. Peter, 'Who is the guy in the white coat?' He looked up, kind of laughed and said, 'Oh, that's God. He thinks he's George Toma.'"

Drive To Perfection

I worked hard at my craft and had an unyielding drive for perfection with every field that I prepared. My no-nonsense style was certainly not for everyone, but perhaps my approach is what allowed me to reach the pinnacle as a groundskeeper.

Chicago is a strict union town. When crews get a break, that's it. No working. But the Teamsters liked the way we worked so much that stadium crews helped us put up a goalpost and lay down a canvas during one of their breaks.

Also while in Chicago, the groundskeepers took me to a family member's home for lunch. Others took me to Armand's Italian Restaurant.

I also tried to give back and share my knowledge. Colleges occasionally invited me as a guest speaker to talk about turf management. But I also took pride in connecting with the common folk.

But not everyone liked my style. I could be tough and difficult, and people said that, too.

Joe Ungashick, who donated his front yard to build a wiffle ball field that raises hundreds of thousands for a wonderful charity, once asked me what the P in George P. Toma stood for.

I told him, "It once stood for prick, but I'm trying to change that."

I've been described as irascible with a Patton style and unbounded energy.

Steadman called me demanding.

Those comments never bothered me. Neither did on-field problems. In fact, I welcomed them, I told Gib Twyman of the Kansas City Star.

"Be thankful for the troubles of your job," I said. "If it were not for the things that go wrong, the difficult people you have to deal with, and the problems and the unpleasantness of your working day, someone could be found to handle your job.

"It takes intelligence, resourcefulness, patience, tact and courage to meet the troubles of any job."

TV Commercials And Pitchman

ESPN had me do one of its famous 30-second SportsCenter commercials.

Wearing a Marquis de Sod T-shirt, I started by saying, "Like a lot of organizations, ESPN was having trouble with its carpet. So they had me install a more natural surface."

Shown above with a group of kids from one of the United Way commercials that I took part in.

The next clips showed what looked like natural grass installed in the hallways and various walkways on the Bristol, Conn., campus. Complete with people mowing and grass blowing.

"This grass we installed is the best," I said. "It's a good Bermuda. Lays down very pretty. Wherever you are, there's nothing more beautiful than grass."

The spot ends with a water sprinkler spraying an office cubicle.

I also endorsed John Deere, Sprite, International Seeds, Pennington Seeds and PBI Gordon Chemicals. There's a large cutout of me in uniform that the Luzerne County Hall of Fame used in an exhibit.

In addition, the United Way had me do a couple of commercials.

Fact And Legend

There have been legendary things said about me, and then there are facts.

> **Fact:** I grew hair on a man's head. A ryegrass toupe. That would be bald-headed Mickey Cobb, the Royals' trainer. And if I do say so myself, he looked pretty good. Made him look 10 years younger.

> **Legend:** I raked children's sand boxes in the greater Kansas City area while they slept at night. They also called me The Sandman.

> **Fact:** While not at the same time, I've worked every minute on the 24-hour clock. Working up to and past midnight was common for Super Bowls. I have worked until 4:30 in the morning, and I've gotten up at 3:30 in the morning to start my day. One time I got some shut-eye in Atlanta Braves star Chipper Jones' locker in the corner after working on the fields for the 1996 Olympics. Another time I slept in

a wheelbarrow. Used a towel for a pillow. Those were two of the best nights of sleep I ever had.

Legend: I could make grass grow by talking to it. Just like people do with plants. Some have called me the grass whisperer.

Fact: I water my own lawn at home. I grow tomatoes, too. Even at 95.

Legend: I could make artificial turf tilt like Emil Bossard did with grass.

Fact: I watered Jack Steadman's wife's convertible – with the top down – as well as trees next to it. Oops.

Legend: I gave lawn tips to the Pope on maintaining the grounds at the Vatican. But I did give lawn tips to Royals Hall of Famer George Brett. He wanted me to go into business with him. We were going to call it "George and George ... for a better swing." I should've done it. Would've made a lot of money.

Legend: Babe Ruth wanted to hire me to secure his footing in the batter's box at Yankee Stadium. Hell, I'm not that old. But shortstop Alex Rodriguez, when he played for the Texas Rangers, asked me to move to Arlington, Texas, to take care of the infield between second and third base.

Fact: I prepared the fields in my backyards where the kids played. Put in lines and everything.

Legendary Encounters

My jobs in the groundskeeping industry have given me the chance to meet so many players, coaches, owners, political leaders and entertainers.

I became friends with many of them. Some of the people you'd think have the biggest egos are the most down-to-earth people. And some people who had questionable talent had out-of-control egos.

Here are some of my favorites:

George Steinbrenner: The former New York Yankees owner was known for his outbursts and firing managers, but he loved talking to the fans. At Baseball City in Haines City, Fla., he'd regularly stay a half-hour after games and chat with kids or their parents. Now, he did accuse me of doctoring a pitching mound when Catfish Hunter pitched, forcing umpires to come early and watch us, but they found nothing. Still, I liked him.

Rush Limbaugh: When the ultraconservative and popular radio talk show host died in 2021, he was worth $600 million, according to reports, but when he worked for the Royals in group sales in the late '70s and early '80s, he barely could rub two pennies together. Constantly, he'd go to the Royals clubhouse and ask for a sandwich. George Brett, who'd become a lifelong friend, bought him a few things. On one of his radio shows, he noted my work ethic, which I appreciated.

George Brett: Great hitter and a dear friend. I was told I needed to protect the lip between third base and dirt because George was our franchise. Sure enough, a ball hit him in the mouth and loosened up a few teeth, but he never blamed me. When he wrote the foreword to *Nitty Gritty Dirt Man* in 2004, he said, "The truth is, George Toma and George Brett are alike in a lot of ways. We couldn't wait to get to the ballpark, and we never wanted to leave. When you have the right attitude, good things can happen."

Dan Quisenberry: The great Royals closer was part of a fun-loving bullpen. The relievers would hose down the fans when they got hot.

Paul McCartney: Even though it was 41 years between the Beatles' concert in Kansas City (1964) and his 2005 Super Bowl performance, he still remembered me. We chatted for a few minutes.

Lady Gaga: When she performed at Super Bowl LI in 2017, before every rehearsal, she'd get on the microphone and thank everyone involved, including the grounds crew. I liked her common touch.

Lenny Dawson: The Kansas City quarterback and long-time studio host for HBO's "Inside the NFL" was a really good man.

Jim Kelly: Before every Super Bowl, the Buffalo Bills quarterback would come down in his pants and T-shirt and tell me a joke. His coach Marv Levy also would come down with his assistants and chat.

Don Shula: The Miami Dolphins coach must have thought I had a lot of influence with 410 Park Avenue. Soldier Field had grass issues, which I tried to fix, and the Dolphins were coming to Chicago for an exhibition game. Shula called me and tried to get the exhibition game canceled. He asked me to talk to the commissioner.

Kevin Stefanski: Before he became the Cleveland Browns' coach, he was a rookie assistant with the Minnesota Vikings. We got to know each other. I'm from Wilkes-Barre, and he's from Philadelphia. We also both like good Polish food. Good kid.

Howie Long: All of the broadcasters came over and asked me about the field, but Howie invited me to dinner at his house. I couldn't because I was working until midnight.

Warren Sapp: After the Tampa Bay Buccaneers won Super Bowl XXXVII in 2003, the defensive tackle picked me up and carried me.

Mark and Zygi Wilf: The Vikings owners were outstanding to me. They paid me five times what the Royals did. In 2006, I received a thank-you letter, and it was hand-delivered.

Smokey Olson: What a character. Montana cowboy. I think he was a hobo, riding the rails. He went to umpire school and didn't make it, so he hung around the Royals, and he used to ride them like a bum. He met women because he liked to dance and play the guitar. When women asked him where he lived, he said, "My bedroom is over the beach." He actually lived in the equipment room by the sand. He said, "My patio is really nice and green." He was talking about the bullpen. And when he said, "I've got a big lawn in my front yard, and many people come to visit me," he was talking about Royals Stadium. When the Milwaukee Brewers were in the American League, Smokey and Bob Uecker would sit in the visiting dugout and tell stories. It was like, "Can you top this?"

Dick Howser: The Royals' manager from 1981 to 1986 and I were very, very close. I knew him when he was a baseball player for Florida State. He won 103 games in 1980, but Steinbrenner let him go. He was going to take the job as Florida State's coach, and he asked me to be the team's groundskeeper. I said, "Dick, let me think it over." In the meantime, the Royals hired him as manager. I told him, "See, if I had taken that job?" When the sports writers came by, he'd often come into my office and relax. In 1985, while the Royals were on their way to winning the World Series, Dick called my uncle John Yarrish – who was like a father to me – and cheered him up while he was in the hospital.

It was really sad that Dick got a brain tumor. I remember him being sick in the hotel at spring training in 1987. He spoke to the team and said he wouldn't be able to manage. He died three months later. On July 3, the Royals retired their first number, and it was Dick's No. 10. Florida State's baseball field is named Mike Martin Field at Dick Howser Stadium. One helluva guy.

Rod Carew, Tony Oliva: A CBS interview showed me and Tony talking. We stayed in touch. When I told the Minnesota Twins I wouldn't be coming down for spring training in 2023, they called me and told me to get my ass down to Fort Myers, Fla.

NFL director of broadcasting Bob Cochran: Before Super Bowl 8 VIII in 1974, the Houston Chronicle did a story on me. Bob was so appreciative, he said, "George Toma should be inducted into the NFL Hall of Fame."

Howard Cosell: He had that cigar, and he walked around the field and asked our grounds crew questions about having all these sports at Municipal Stadium. Mike Swanson, who used to cut grass for me, retired from the Royals as promotions director. Howard hired him as a spotter.

Honor Of A Lifetime

Turned out that Bob was quite the prognosticator as that day happened 27 years later.

Below is the letter I received from the Pro Football Hall of Fame in 2001 welcoming me to Canton as a recipient of the Hall's Ralph Hay Pioneer Award.

Pro Football Hall of Fame

George Toma
May 23, 2001

You are receiving this award for your many years of service to the National Football League in the expert preparation, care and enhancement of its championship game field, including all 35 Super Bowls. Your ability to revive, create, and maintain field surfaces in the safest manner is legendary and unmatched.

As I mentioned, the award will be given to you Friday morning, August 3, 2001 here in Canton, Ohio at the Mayor's Breakfast, before an audience of 4,000. The class of 2001 and approximately 40 other Hall of Famers will also be recognized at that event.

Due to the length of the program, you will only have a minute for your acceptance of the award.

You and your wife, Donna, will be guests of the Pro Football Hall of Fame. You will need to arrive Thursday afternoon, so that you can attend the Board of Trustees Reception that night. We would hope that you would stay for the Enshrinees' Civic Dinner Friday night and the enshrinement on Saturday, the 4th. Tammy Owens, of our staff, will be in touch with you on your air travel and hotel accommodations as well as event tickets. She will go over the enclosed reservation form with you.

Again, we congratulate you on this very deserving recognition and look forward to having you and Donna here in Canton for this occasion.

Sincerely,

John Bankert
Executive Director

Cc: Jim Steeg
Val Pinchbeck

I had so many people to thank and so little time, but I made my minute count with this acceptance speech:

Thank you. Honored guests, ladies and gentlemen.

What a surprise, some 60 years ago, from marking football fields in the anthracite coal region of Edwardsville, Pennsylvania, with screened white coal ashes and black coal dust on a snow-covered field.

Here I am today, unbelievable. It would not have happened without the help of my family, Mr. Lamar Hunt, Jack Steadman, a sincere special thanks to

Commissioner Pete Rozelle, Tex Schramm, the Hall of Fame Committee, and all those people who have worked with me.

Every blade of grass has an angel bending over it, whispering grow, grow; I'm like a blade of grass with so many saints helping me along the way.

A very sincere special thanks to Commissioner Paul Tagliabue, my six all-pro quarterbacks who I was a recipient of their touchdown passes of help – Bill Granholm, Val Pinchbeck, Don Weiss, Roger Goodell, Joe Brown, agronomist Dr. James R. Watson, and in today's materialistic world, a man who has not lost the common touch, my coach and NFL father, Jim Steeg. Yes, Jim, the NFL shield will be with me always and over my heart.

To the NFL and Pro Football Hall of Fame, may all of you be repaid a thousandfold for your kindness, and to all of you, may all your good fortunes be as numerous as blades of grass, seed, the gift of life.

Yes, in God we trust.

10

Tricks Of The Trade

"An inch is often the difference between a base hit and an out. We try to have the inches go our way."

– Legendary groundskeeper Emil Bossard

Whenever I had a problem related to groundskeeping, I had a friendly voice I always could call.

Emil Bossard, the greatest groundskeeper ever. He was called "Doctor of the Diamond."

I was lucky.

That thought lingered with me when I met with some of the finest people in our profession in 1981. We talked about starting an organization.

Joining me were Harry Gill, groundskeeper of the Milwaukee Brewers; Dr. William Daniel, an agronomist at Purdue; and Dick Ericson, a groundskeeper for the Minnesota Vikings and Twins.

Kansas City played host to the Parks and Recreation Convention, and after the festivities, we went for a drink at historic Hotel Muehlebach.

"We should have an organization that can help people if

you are a groundskeeper," I told the men. "Maybe we should go through all levels of sports, Little League and youth sports to the pros. Give everyone a safe playing field and give everyone a way to call one another and help one another."

Gill and Daniel led the way. Ericson and I came up with ideas. I really admired Dick because of all the snow and ice he had to deal with at Metropolitan Stadium.

Within a few months, we had developed the Sports Turf Managers Association. Now called the Sports Field Management Association, it aims to advance professionalism in sports field management and safety through education, awareness programs, and industry development.

My Mentor

Unfortunately, Emil Bossard wasn't around to see the formation of our association. He died in 1980.

Emil Bossard was born in Switzerland in 1891. According to a biography the Arizona Daily Star's David Leighton wrote, Emil's family immigrated to the United States when he was only 1, ultimately settling in St. Paul, Minn.

Emil – a naturalized citizen of the United States in 1908 – had been working as a laborer when he landed a job in 1915 as groundskeeper for the St. Paul Saints minor league baseball team.

The Saints now are the Triple-A affiliate of the Minnesota Twins. The Saints have had many lives.

They began in 1884. A second incarnation lasted from 1894 to 1899 and became a forerunner to the Chicago White Sox. Incarnation No. 3 came from 1915 to 1960 as a member of the American Association.

After a 33-year absence, the Saints were revived where they were an independent team with no Major League Baseball affiliation. They played in the Northern League from 1993 to 2005 and the American Association of Independent Professional Baseball from 2006 to 2020.

In 2021, the Saints became MLB affiliated, and they now are part of the International League.

Me and my mentor Emil Bossard, who I consider to be the GGOAT - Greatest Groundskeeper Of All Time.

Emil claimed he didn't know a lot about groundskeeping at first, but he sure became a quick learner.

He stayed with the Saints until becoming head groundskeeper with the Cleveland Indians in 1936.

That was the same year Joe DiMaggio started his career with the Yankees.

"We hated (visiting Cleveland) because our every defensive flaw was exploited by the Bossards the way they prepared the playing field," DiMaggio said in a story written by John Kmitta of SportsField Management.

Indians manager Lou Boudreau called Emil "the 10th man in our lineup."

Emil did give the Indians an edge.

Based on what the Indians wanted, he'd:

Tilt the base lines in or out, so balls were more likely to roll fair or foul.

Water the base paths to slow down opposing runners if they had the faster team or dry them if Cleveland liked to steal bases.

Adjust the height cut on the infield grass to impact the speed of ground balls.

Soak or harden the ground in front of the plate depending on whether a sinker ball pitcher was on the mound for the Indians or their opponent.

Emil recalled he often took orders.

"(Second baseman) Bobby Avila wanted me to tilt the base paths so his bunts wouldn't roll out. (Manager/shortstop) Lou Boudreau wanted me to soak the hell out of the field. (Second baseman) Joe Gordon wanted it the opposite ... and (third baseman) Kenny Keltner wanted the field to be solid so the ball would come right to him. And with Bill Veeck, we used to move in the fences, but you can't do that during the season now."

The last world championship the Indians, now called the Guardians, won in 1948, came when Emil performed more of his magic. To show their appreciation, the players gave him a World Series share and bought him a Buick. Mr. Bossard would then use the car's tires to roll the infield dirt.

However, Emil was much more than that. He was an inventor. He came up with the nail drag, an edging shovel, rakes, and practices such as soaking clay in a bathtub. He devised a drainage system where his concepts still are used today. His hand seeding rivaled any mechanical seeder seen today. Emil would take a bucket, put seed in it, and scatter the seed with his hands. He taught us to push and pull to rake the seed into the soil.

And he was an artist. Emil painted using a 4-inch paintbrush, which created sharp lines. He used bailing wire instead of string to lay out the arc.

When Bill Veeck became the Cleveland Indians owner in 1946, he promoted me to head groundskeeper in Wilkes-Barre, then sent me to work with Emil Bossard.

I went through grade school and high school, and Emil was the best teacher I ever had. It was like being taught football by Vince Lombardi or baseball by Connie Mack. A.L. Hardman wrote of some of the tricks of the trade I learned in the Charleston Gazette.

He took me aside like one of his family.

In 1950, Emil Bossard, right, and me built six fields at the old Daytona Beach Naval Air Station.

I also helped Mr. Bossard as we built fields during the 1940s and 1950s on military bases that were decommissioned after World War II. Stan Schlecker, who helped me get my start in the business, also joined us.

We worked at a naval air station in Virginia in 1948, then again on an Air Force base in Georgia in 1949.

In 1950, we built six fields at the old Daytona Beach Naval Air Station. And we did this without modern equipment or engineered soil mixes. We'd just find infield dirt and then work the soil. That's why Emil invented the nail drag.

The man could close his eyes, use his imagination and create a field better than anyone I ever have known.

Emil also:

Installed an electronic sprinkling system at Hi Corbett Field in Tucson, Ariz., in December 1958.

Built a new type of automatic pitching machine capable of throwing a baseball faster than any human pitcher.

Helped the Indians become the first major-league team to have two official spring-training fields when the annex field behind the right-field wall of Hi Corbett Field was made into the second official field.

On Jan. 19, 1959, the Tucson Daily Citizen said Emil had been "rated unanimously as the No. 1 groundskeeper in all of baseball."

Two years later, he retired as the Indians' chief groundskeeper and was replaced by his son Harold. Sons Marshall and Gene also became groundskeepers.

In the 1970s, Emil worked as a consultant for several different ball parks, including Hi Corbett Field. Those annex fields now are called the Emil Bossard Annex Fields.

Emil's son Gene was the White Sox's head groundskeeper at old Comiskey from 1940 to 1983, one of the longest tenures by anyone in the field.

Roger Bossard, Gene's son, also made a name for himself. He joined the White Sox in 1967 working as an assistant to his father before becoming the official head groundskeeper. "The Sodfather II" has played a big role in the development of new ballparks and is the longest-tenured groundskeeper in major-league history. He also has been with the Sox longer than any other employee.

In 1984, he was hired by a member of the Saudi royal family to build the first-ever natural-turf soccer field in the desert. He filled two jumbo jets with California sod and flew it overseas. With the help of a desalination unit to rid the grass of salty sand and a double-irrigation system to provide plenty of water, he made the soccer field happen, according to writer Mike Thomas.

Nineteen of 30 major-league teams use a patented drainage system that Roger developed for the opening of Guaranteed Rate Field in 1991, including Arizona's Chase Field, Detroit's Comerica Park, Milwaukee's American Family Field, St. Louis' Busch Stadium, Seattle's T-Mobile

Park, Washington's Nationals Park, Chicago's Wrigley Field and spring training complexes for the Cincinnati Reds, Montreal Expos, New York Yankees, St. Louis Cardinals, Arizona Diamondbacks, Los Angeles Dodgers and Chicago White Sox.

Grandson Brian, great-grandson James and great-great-grandson Andrew all carry on the legacy started by Emil.

That means the Bossard family has had professional groundskeepers for more than 110 years.

I have worked with Brian in Super Bowls and have gotten to know the others, and they're all outstanding.

We all went to Cooperstown and shed a tear when Emil was inducted posthumously into the Baseball Hall of Fame on Jan. 8, 2012.

Groundskeeping By Deceit

I used some of Emil's tricks while adding some of my own when opposing players came into town.

One time, I tried cutting the grass in four different patterns to see if that was how the truest roll could be obtained. I also considered circular cuts from mowing around the edge of the infield, down one foul line, around the edge of the outfield and then back down the other foul line. The mowing would continue in consecutive smaller circles.

I'd regularly meet with manager Alvin Dark to go over field strategy. Sometimes, he left it up to the players to tell me the way they wanted their part of the diamond manicured.

After reading a book that detailed how Ted Williams liked a soft batter's box, we made it like concrete. Williams hated to hit at Municipal Stadium because he couldn't get a toehold. We'd put in extra clay and tamp it down hard.

We did something similar with Wade Boggs. But for George Brett, there was soft dirt at the precise spot where he dug in.

We also made the center field hard as a rock when Mickey Mantle came into town. Same at third base when

Baltimore's Brooks Robinson visited. He couldn't glove what he couldn't reach.

If our team faced a fastball pitcher, I moved the batter's box back six inches. If the pitcher threw a lot of sinker balls, we made the ground hard. Royals manager Hal McRae used to shake my hand if a player got a hit that bounced past the infielders.

Opposing players would get even with me. White Sox second baseman Nellie Fox used to go out behind Municipal Stadium and collect golf-ball-sized rocks and hide them under second base. He'd then toss them into the crowd to embarrass me.

Ed Short of the White Sox didn't like that we had the infield grass high, which almost nullified his team's chances of bunting.

"When is Charlie Finley going to buy you a lawnmower?" Short asked.

I replied, "OK, you buy me a lawnmower, and I'll buy you a truckload of dirt to build up your baselines."

Short got the point.

For the most part, we had good banter with opposing players. It was nothing illegal. We were just trying to help our team a little bit.

In 1966, the Baltimore Orioles clinched the American League pennant against the Athletics in Kansas City.

Dick Mackay of the Kansas City Star wrote that Orioles manager Hank Bauer cornered me and growled, "We could have lost the pennant here ... the way you doctored up around home plate."

I responded, "But Hank, you taught me how to do it."

Bauer gave a double take, then smiled and walked away. He couldn't be too mad at me. I helped prolong his career with some of the field doctoring I did, softening right field for him.

In a 1994 interview with Dick Kaegel of the Kansas City star, I said, "Hank Bauer used to say I was the 10th man on the club down at old Municipal. They call it groundskeeping by deceit."

Jim "Catfish" Hunter

Jim Hunter grew up with me and the Kansas City Athletics.

When Catfish lost one of his toes to a hunting accident and needed time to recover, many scouts shied away from him, but Charles O. Finley didn't and signed him to a contract. Because he was 16 at the time, Hunter hung out with my grounds crew because a lot of the guys were his age. Mr. Finley preferred that to him hanging out with the older ballplayers where he could develop bad habits.

Melvin Duncan, one of my best groundskeepers, didn't grow up with a lot of meat in his household, so his mother fed him tongue sandwiches. Cow tongue sandwiches. Melvin started giving some of his cow tongue sandwiches to Catfish.

"He said, 'That's some good beef,' and ate it three, four, five, six times," Melvin said. "When I told him what it was, he said, 'That was what? Oh, no.'"

Mr. Finley flew Catfish and me up to his farm in Laporte, Ind. As you drive toward the farm, you see a big, white barn with a green A's logo painted on it.

The farm had cattle and corn on it – as well as a swimming pool.

Hunter became a bit of a legend. Finley, thinking he needed a nickname for the right-hander, started calling him Catfish in 1965, even though he never caught a catfish.

Still, singer Bob Dylan used his name in one of his songs. Walter Matthau uttered his name in a couple of films he did.

Despite skipping the minors aside from a stint in the Florida Instructional League, Hunter made the American League all-star teams in 1966 and '67. In 1968, he threw the ninth perfect game in major league history.

After he helped the A's win three World Series titles in the early 1970s, the New York Yankees signed him as a free agent in 1974.

In the 1976 American League Championship Series between the Yankees and Royals, Hunter started Game 1. The day before the game, he complained because he didn't have a lot of success at Royals Stadium.

"Every time I go out there, (Toma) has two inches of mud on the mound," Catfish told a New York newspaper. "Then you combine that artificial surface with the wet mound and it's almost impossible to pitch out there."

Melvin Duncan, who worked on the mound, knew Catfish liked a hard mound and hard rubber, so he softened it. When Catfish asked him about it, Melvin said, "I guess we watered it too much.

"We've really fixed it up for him."

Did we use gamesmanship? Probably.

The definition of gamesmanship is: the art of winning games by using various ploys and tactics to gain a psychological advantage.

Yeah, that about sums it up.

For Game 1, our crew was watched all day, starting at 8 a.m. Billy Martin and George Steinbrenner had umpires from MLB out there for hours before the game. Steinbrenner could be seen walking down the first base and right-field line. Funny thing is, Martin used similar tricks as a manager.

I laughed at Catfish's remarks.

"More than anything, this is a psychological thing," I told the media. "I could tell him I've really fixed the mound up, and even if I hadn't, he would be thinking about how bad it was.

"We're not doing anything illegal. Our mound specs meet MLB criteria. In the early days, he gave me some of the credit for his success. He relies a great deal on the shape and condition of the mound. I did my best to help him when he was here. Now, I do whatever I can to hinder him."

To Hunter's credit, he pitched a complete-game five-hitter in a 4-1 win. The Yankees won the series.

"He pitched well," Melvin said. "He just moved over on the mound a few inches."

SFMA

Today, the Sports Field Management Association has about 3,000 members. There are five officers and eight directors.

Everyone can be an active member, as there are 24 committees ranging from advocacy to technology.

I thought Kim Heck – the former SFMA CEO for 18 years – did a good job. I knew her when she was a Kansas City Chiefette.

"He's definitely an expert in his field," Kim said. "When someone is an expert, we also look to them for leadership. Their expertise gives them a lot more weight."

Every January, the SFMA has a four-day conference and exhibition.

Over the years, I have advocated two main tenets.

The best insurance for an athlete at all levels is a safe playing field.

When doing work on a field, do your best – and then some.

"He's great in the spotlight," Kim said. "He's helped the association and our foundation. When we auction items, George will rip off his shirt or donate items."

The SFMA has continued to honor me with the George Toma Golden Rake Award. It acknowledges the superior performance of a sports turf crew member in on-the-job activities and in community service.

I tried to emphasize that there's no George Toma without the people I worked for. I often said, "My crew never worked for me, they worked with me."

I also came across this poem I shared:

I've always been for the underdog
I like to see him win,
For he is almost always on
The outside looking in.

True, I respect a winner
They rate a second glance,
But I'm the one who likes to give
The other guy a chance.

Of course, when someone hits the top
They try real hard to stay,
And this practice will be so
However rough the way.

It's the same industry, sports and the turf world
The big shadows, the small.
Everyone delights to rise
None relishes a fall.

Yet, I am for the underdog
Who strives to make the grade,
I supposed it's human nature
The mold from which he's made.

When we had some problems, I wrote an open letter to SFMA members in July of 2003.

In it, I said, "This is your organization and we need to let bygones be bygones and pull together.

"Until the rake is plied from my cold, dead fingers I always will try to help dedicated groundskeepers from preschool to the professional ranks do the job, attain respect on all levels, and then some, which distinguishes the great from the mediocre."

In 2011, I wrote my farewell column for SportsField Management.

I wrote, To all the groundskeepers who love me – or who hate me – I've always tried to tell it as it is, pulling no punches. People think I give them hell, but I just tell the truth.

A number of groundskeepers and NFL officials wrote letters, which shared how much they learned but also how much they enjoyed working with me.

"He's really stressed working hard and having fun, and he's led the way in both," wrote Heather Nabozny, the Detroit Tigers' head groundskeeper.

Steve Wightman, who retired in 2012 after almost 40 years

in the business, did a wonderful job of bringing everyone in the organization together. People who acted like politicians – their asses were out.

Now, we're one, big happy family.

This organization makes me proud.

I'd like to think Emil Bossard from his perch in heaven would say something like, "Good job, kid."

11

The Flood, The Field, The Catch

"By the end of the 1981 regular season, the
field was a mess. I told the parks department
the grounds crew had to get it right
for this biggest of playoff games."

- Former San Francisco mayor Dianne Feinstein
to *The Game Before the Money Podcast*

Besides Super Bowls, the NFL occasionally had me work on fields for playoff games.

The toughest field I ever prepared was for the 1981 season's NFC championship game between the San Francisco 49ers and Dallas Cowboys. I told Cedar Rapids Gazette columnist Bob Denney, "It looked like a World War II mine field."

When the Midwest gets a winter storm, it's called a blizzard. But when San Francisco got a winter storm, the government declared it a disaster area.

From Jan. 3 to 5, 1982, as much as 16 inches of rain fell in Marin County and 25 inches in the mountains bordering

Santa Cruz County. For a period of time, the Golden Gate Bridge was closed.

The most severe damage occurred in the hills and coastal ranges around the San Francisco Bay Area where flooding, mudslides, and debris flows destroyed many homes and businesses. Joint federal and state damage estimates indicated that 6,300 residences were damaged, of which 231 were destroyed. Lives also were lost.

Shortly after I arrived, Dianne Feinstein – then mayor of San Francisco – greeted me. Because of the drainage problems, players often called the field "The Quag" – short for quagmire. It didn't help that Candlestick Park was only about 14 feet above sea level.

"George, what can we do?" she said.

Regularly during the week, the mayor came down in her boots, rain hat and coat.

Anything I needed was available to me. I worked with Barney Barron, director of parks and recreation; Jim Lucy; and John Wurm. They were great people.

The 49ers had beaten the New York Giants a few days earlier in the NFC divisional round, so the field had taken a beating. After the game, the 49ers traveled to Anaheim – 408 miles away – for midweek practices.

"It's still a horse-bleep field," Giants coach Ray Perkins said, and 49ers linebacker Jack "Hacksaw" Reynolds added, "It's like playing in swampland."

Over the next few days, the field had gotten about 6½ inches of rain, a fraction of the precipitation that fell in nearby areas.

But still a lot of rain.

I originally wanted to use Warren's Turf Farm sod, which produced beautiful blue grass. We would cut 18-by-36-inch strips and lay them down at the center of the field. However, Warren's Turf Farm couldn't cut the sod for us.

After talking with Feinstein and the parks and recreation staff, we turned to Kezar Stadium, the site where the 49ers and Cowboys met in the 1970 season's NFC championship game.

Kezar Stadium had Kikuyu grass, a tough, low-growing perennial grass with an extensive network of coarse-creeping stems. It was introduced to California to control erosion on hillsides.

I thought of it as a beautiful weed.

We took 18-by-42-inch strips, put them on plyboard to carry and laid them down in the center of the field. We also laid down a material called Enkamat, a nylon netting about a half-inch thick that looks like several piled layers of chain-link fence, on the field's underlying sand.

When the media got wind of what we were doing, the critics came out. They already had given a hard time to the grounds crew, which they derisively called "The Sod Squad."

Stephen Cockerham, one of the top agronomists on the West Coast, said, "(Toma) doesn't know what he's doing. It's going to be a mess."

I didn't get along well with agronomists. They had a book on how to grow grass, and I didn't go by their book.

What I've done my whole career worked then, and it works now.

The field held up well.

We had every inch of that playing field in good shape – and we needed to.

The game is known for "The Catch." With 51 seconds left, Joe Montana could push off his back foot on the turf to find Dwight Clark in the back of the end zone for a touchdown.

San Francisco won 28-27 on Jan. 10, days after that massive rainstorm.

What amazed people is how high Clark reached up to catch that ball. If that's a soft or mushy field, he just can't jump that high.

After the game, former Kansas City Chiefs coach Hank Stram – who worked the game with Vin Scully for CBS – called the field maintenance a "miraculous job."

But he also said he wasn't surprised.

"A couple of days before a game, George would say, 'Hey Coach, you want a slow field or a fast field?' " Stram said.

Even though the Cowboys lost, general manager Tex Schramm said, "George really turned that field around. But that's not surprising. George is a creative man. I've really admired his advanced thinking in a lot of areas, especially painting the field. Nobody does it the way George Toma does."

I didn't think the effort was my best, but a lot of other people did. And Mayor Feinstein was quite pleased.

Maybe the mayor liked what I said about her because everyone in the press wanted to give me credit for making Candlestick Park look so great in 1982 but I deferred to her.

"I want no credit," I said. "That lady in her raincoat and her muddy boots, constantly asking us what do we need – she's the one who deserves the credit."

After the game at Candlestick Park, I was focused on preparing the Silverdome in Pontiac, Mich., for the Super Bowl. Our crew went over every inch of the artificial turf, checking seams and repairing them.

After I suggested San Francisco needed a football grounds crew 365 days a year, the mayor and city officials wanted to hire me despite my critical comments. They talked to me during Super Bowl XVI, then offered the job.

I strongly considered the position, not just because sports reporter Mike McKenzie said I'd be paid twice as much but because turning that field around would be the biggest challenge a person in my profession could have.

On Jan. 27 – three days after Super Bowl XVI – the lead story in the Kansas City Times was Bob Gretz's report on Mayor Feinstein wanting me to work for the San Francisco 49ers and Giants.

"She says she is going to sign me as a free agent," I was quoted as saying.

Royals and Chiefs executives Herk Robinson and Jack Steadman didn't know of San Francisco's offer until the Kansas City Times contacted them.

"I would certainly hope he would sit down and visit with us and the Royals if he is considering a move," Steadman said. "I'm sure he gets a lot of offers. He'd be hard to replace.

Hopefully, we won't have to replace him. He does well financially with our two organizations."

Robinson added, "He's a very talented groundskeeper and has done an excellent job in Kansas City. I'm certain he has had several offers over the years, but he has always chosen to stay here. He has been very happy here. He's challenged by the two stadiums."

In the story, Billy Granholm, special assistant to the NFL, also complimented me.

"We use George because there is nobody in his business that is better," he said. "George has tremendous pride in what he does. He's a complete workaholic and highly organized."

Mayor Feinstein really put the push on. She put on a party for me after I returned from the Jan. 31 Pro Bowl in Hawaii. I was gifted with sourdough bread, cheeses and meats.

While I loved Kansas City, I had to think about it.

San Francisco made a great offer.

But I chose to stay in Kansas City.

When the media asked why, I said I really didn't know.

But I did. I just didn't like the idea of living in a big city. It's why I turned down the New York Yankees. And it's why I turned down the California Angels. Angels owner Gene Autry and I had many conversations. One time, we sat in the Royals' dugout and he showed me pictures of houses.

California was just too big.

The Royals and Chiefs, knowing how much I enjoyed living in Kansas City, didn't overwhelm me with an offer to stay.

When it's winter time, they offer you ice cubes.

Return To San Francisco

About 11 years later, I was back in San Francisco for another 49ers-Cowboys NFC championship game. Similar problem: more rain the week of the game. Writer Michael Madden said the two biggest storylines seemed to be the turf and the haircuts of Cowboys coach Jimmy Johnson and 49ers coach George Seifert.

USA Today's Erik Brady began his story with a twist on a popular poem:

George be nimble,
George be quick,
George make over
The Candlestick

We brought sod from Indio in the Southern California desert. A new company called West Coast Turf. Strips of Bermuda overseeded with rye were laid in 36-foot pieces with 36 pencil-sized holes punched in each square foot to aid drainage.

We had to put in 19-hour days as we sodded the field. I told the media, "Right now, I'd say it's the best playing surface in the NFL."

Less than 48 hours before the title game, an earthquake struck Northern California. It registered up to 5.7 on the Richter scale. But we were focused on Candlestick.

Sunday was foggy and the field a bit muddy, but CBS' Pat Summerall opened by saying, "They've done a heck of a job."

The field didn't look the best from a TV aesthetics standpoint – the green in the middle of the field was different than that on the outside – but the footing was outstanding. Late in the game during a timeout, CBS cameras caught me touching up the white lines in the field of play.

After the game, Seifert said, "The field certainly was better than last week. The grounds crew did a wonderful job. It was in better shape than we expected it to be."

The Cowboys, who won 30-20, also were complimentary.

"Everybody talked so much about the field conditions and how everyone was going to be sliding around," quarterback Troy Aikman said. "As it turned out, the field conditions weren't that bad."

Offensive lineman Nate Newton added, "The field was great. Thank God for the field doctor."

I also received a note from the commissioner.

January 19, 1993

Dear George:

Just a note of gratitude for the superb job you performed on the Candlestick field for the NFC Championship Game.

We deeply appreciate your commitment and extraordinary efforts to provide the best possible playing fields for NFL events. Under the circumstances, the job you did last week was truly remarkable.

I look forward to seeing you in Pasadena and at the Pro Bowl.

Best regards,
Paul Tagliabue

Tip Of The Cap

On Sept. 29, 2023, Dianne Feinstein died at the age of 90. After becoming Mayor Feinstein, she became U.S. Senator Feinstein and held that position from 1992 to 2023. She became the longest-serving woman senator in U.S. history.

Echoing many others, Vice President Kamala Harris called Feinstein "one of the greatest public servants that California and our nation has ever known."

I really admired that lady in the raincoat and muddy boots.

There were more than a few people I wanted to send to Washington, D.C., for a conversation with that lady on leadership.

Former NFL commissioner Paul Tagliabue and me.

12

Taming Mother Nature

"Neither snow nor rain nor heat nor gloom of night stays these couriers from the swift completion of their appointed rounds."

- *The Persian Wars*, Herodotus

The excessive rains in the days leading up to those classic Dallas Cowboys-San Francisco 49ers NFC championship games were just a couple of examples of the excessive rain the crew and I had to deal with.

In fact, they were just a couple of examples of major weather problems we faced before Super Bowls, playoff games, and regular-season contests. Those included:

Hurricanes
Tornadoes
Rain
Flooding
Snow
Freezing cold
Blistering heat

Here are the most challenging weather scenarios I dealt with over the course of my career.

Tornadoes And Cold

Preparations for Super Bowl IV in Tulane Stadium in 1970 had a strange mix of weather.

During the week, we had tornado warnings.

The day of the game we experienced a cold, wet field. It was so cold that the water in the restrooms froze.

Because we didn't have much warm weather, we couldn't do much about the little to no grass in the end zones.

The best I could do was lay down sawdust and wood chips, which we painted over.

While it was wet in spots, the footing held well.

150-Degree Heat

Former Kansas City second baseman Frank White once saw me cook an egg on the AstroTurf field at Royals Stadium. Surface temperatures would get incredibly hot.

Kansas City could be one of the hottest places in the country during the summer, and the artificial turf made the field hotter. Royals executive Herk Robinson wouldn't let us put thermometers on the field, but the players brought their own. We checked the field temperature, and more than once it was 150 degrees. Or hotter.

After the Royals jogged to the dugout following their turn on the field, they put their cleats in wooden trays filled with ice. You could almost hear the sizzle. You could see the heat radiating from the turf.

Players tried to get even with the field. Back then, players chewed tobacco and they spit and stained the field. Others chewed bubble gum and sometimes left their wads on the field. Others wrapped their bubble gum around a wad of tobacco and put it in their mouths.

I think they did it because it kept their mouths moist and the chewing relaxed them.

It made our jobs tougher. While the tobacco juice stained

the field and needed to be cleaned with ammonia, we needed gum freeze and special combs to take the bubble gum out.

Cold And Wind

I didn't work the Ice Bowl between the Green Bay Packers and Dallas Cowboys in 1967, but I did work a couple of freezing games.

The coldest I ever felt was in Chicago for Bears playoff games in the 1980s.

Chicago's Soldier Field, the coldest I ever got for an NFL game.

I was there at the request of Mike Ditka, a good friend of mine. For those frigid games, one of the things we tried to do was cover the field with canvas, then blow hot air underneath.

Late-night TV host Johnny Carson had this line: "It was so cold ..." Well, it was so cold and so windy for the Bears' divisional playoff game against the New York Giants in the 1985 season that punter Sean Landeta almost completely whiffed his punt while kicking from his end zone. The Bears picked up the ball and scored a touchdown.

Fortunately, temperatures were in the 30s that day. Just 13 days later, the temps plummeted to 27 below with a minus 70 wind chill in some areas.

Hurricanes

While building practice fields in Jacksonville for Super Bowl XXXIX, I dealt with four hurricanes in 2004: Charley, Frances, Ivan, and Jeanne. Those four storms caused an estimated $50 billion in damage.

Since hurricane records started being kept in the 1850s, it was the only time that four hurricanes hit the state of Florida in one year.

They made prepping those fields challenging in August and September. One field looked great, but the other one felt like concrete. We had to re-loosen it by aerifying and grading it.

Rain

Rain constantly was a factor over the years, but one of the worst times was before Super Bowl XXVII at the Rose Bowl in January 1993.

Almost 15 inches of rain fell in a 14-day span, forcing us to reseed. We used International seeds from Halsey, Ore.

Legendary broadcaster John Madden said it would be less of a factor than the previous week because I'd be able to get 20 hours of good work in.

Most football fields should be cut between one-half and

Bundled up and ready to face the elements with a rake in one hand and a shovel in the other.

three-quarters of an inch, but the Rose Bowl was at seven-eighths because of the turf's wetness.

We used Derby, Regal and Gator grasses as well as the PhD mix. Conditions were idyllic on game day. The grass looked terrific, and the colors popped on television.

Snow

The Farmer's Almanac predicted a blizzard for Super Bowl XLVII at MetLife Stadium in New Jersey in 2014.

While it wasn't that bad, we did get a lot of snow. We had a heated tent over us while we applied the paint at midfield and in the end zones.

The New York Giants' grounds crew, led by Rob Davis, was on top of it. He'd be outside, no hat on, pushing snow off the sidelines. He also brought me kielbasa every other day. What a treat.

Someone who could appreciate the different conditions I worked in was referee Red Cashion, who officiated NFL games from 1972 to 1996 and worked two Super Bowls. He was known for his "first dowwwnnn" call.

February 8, 1999

Mr. George Toma,

Congratulations George, on another great Super Bowl! I had several fans at my home watching and about midway through the 2nd quarter, they began to discuss the field. They could not believe the condition the field was in and how well it was holding up.

With a great deal of pleasure, I told them about you and how much the NFL depended on your skills for all of the big games.

George, I miss seeing you and I hope we can get together sometime. Congratulations again on another great year.

Red Cashion

13

Have Rake, Will Travel

"He's here, he's there, he's every f—ing where!"

- Roy Kent chant in the TV series Ted Lasso

My groundskeeping consulting work took me to numerous countries as well as about half the states in America.

In Florida, I worked in cities coast-to-coast, including Pensacola, Tallahassee, Jacksonville, Daytona Beach, Tampa, Haines City, Avon Park, Fort Lauderdale, Fort Myers, and Miami.

In California, I went to San Diego, Pasadena, Los Angeles, Oakland, and San Francisco.

When I worked the Olympics and World Cup, I traveled to Atlanta; Foxborough, Mass.; and L.A.

Sometimes when I had these big jobs to do and I completed them, I sat back and thought about how I got the job done.

Honestly, our Lord Jesus Christ and the Holy Mary, mother of God, helped me. I also said a prayer to my guardian angel.

Here are some of my favorite experiences:

Hawaii

I worked 35 Pro Bowls at Aloha Stadium in Honolulu, Hawaii. The NFL played there every year from 1980 to 2016, except for 2010 and 2015.

The people treated me well. I told reporter Bill Kwon of the Honolulu Star-Advertiser, "Those people at Aloha Stadium are as good as anybody." I still hear from them every Christmas, and they send me Hawaiian coffee and macadamia nuts.

When I first arrived in January 1980 and people heard the name Toma, they looked for a Japanese guy. Same thing when I went to Tokyo. I had to explain I was Ukrainian.

However, I was treated as one of their own. Members of the state Senate signed and presented me with a certificate that read, "Aloha and mahalo for your years of dedicated service to professional baseball and football and for your contribution to the NFC/AFC Pro Bowl in Honolulu, Hawaii."

Pictured from left to right: Me, Lilian Komatsubara, Walter Komatsubara and my wife Donna Toma on one of our many trips to Hawaii.

Donna and the kids always enjoyed Hawaii because the NFL told us to stay over there for an extra week on its dime. Getting out of Kansas City to spend time in Honolulu in February was a pretty good deal.

There also were a couple of projects that I worked on.

In 2001, I went to Maui to rectify unsafe field conditions at War Memorial Stadium in Wailuku. A lot of teams played high school football there. The University of Hawaii also was scheduled to play Montana at the stadium.

Using our pre-germination method, we turned that field from dead grass into a nice-looking playing surface in 12 days, I told Timothy Hurley with the Star-Advertiser.

Hawaii coach June Jones said if he gave out a game ball, I would've received one.

In another project, in 2003, we needed 450 tons of sand brought in from China to make two practice football fields and a soccer field for the University of Hawaii.

Pierre Alarie was a perfectionist as we reworked Aloha Stadium with his movable trays and cut rubber geo tile mats while combining drainage and glue to fit it all together. I learned a lot from the Hawaiian people.

For years, they moved four huge sections of their stadium on a cushion of air to change a field from baseball to football. It was amazing to watch. Experts from the mainland came to help out. And when the stadium sections wouldn't move, they put tea leaves down all around the stadium wall. In a day or two they moved. They told me they had to satisfy the spirits.

With a cigarette hanging out of the side of his mouth, George Ishikawa quietly painted lines. When he spoke, he talked of being a tunnel rat in the Vietnam War. Viet Cong tunnel networks caused U.S. soldiers a lot of problems, and few Americans could fit into the tunnels and follow the guerrillas to their bases. Tunnel rats volunteered for the dangerous duty. Next to helicopter pilots and long-range reconnaissance patrols, few soldiers put themselves in harm's way as much as the tunnel rats.

Walter Komatsubara, who died in 2010 at 81, was a retired

Honolulu fire captain and a professional baseball scout for the Boston Red Sox. Like me, he was an Army veteran who served in the Korean War. Walter had a philosophy of helping someone when they needed it and asking for nothing in return.

1984 Olympics

Peter Ueberroth, chairman of the Los Angeles Olympic Organizing Committee, called me to serve because the Rose Bowl grass died 23 days before the start of the soccer tournament.

I told a reporter it looked like "Grandma's quilt."

When reporter Eric Adler asked me about the turf, I said, "It's dead. That's why I'm here."

Ueberroth told me, "George, I don't give a darn if you have to go to the South Pacific for fertilizer or if you have to put grow lights up. We have to have this field ready. FIFA is worried."

We put in 200 tons of sand to top-dress it, overseeded and aerified that Bermuda, and it came out great.

Ueberroth thanked me, and we became good friends.

1989 Japan Bowl

I went to Japan for a 10-day trip in 1989 to prepare the practice and game fields for the Japan Bowl, which was a postseason college football all-star game played each January from 1976 to 1993. While I was there, a person I got to know well talked about me while being interviewed by Kent Pulliam of the Kansas City Star.

"He's concentrating on the practice sites. He's overseeing that (resodding) and will lend his expertise on placing the goal posts and marking the field. We were concerned about making the arrangements over there and seeing if they were going to need any NFL assistance. Once we were over there and discovered that they did, we immediately thought of George because of our past relationship with him."

The person quoted was Roger Goodell. At the time, he was the assistant to the president of the AFC.

I'm surrounded by a talented team of groundkeepers that I supervised in preparing football fields in Japan in 1989.

Barcelona, 1993

I arrived six weeks ahead of the Aug. 1, 1993, game between the San Francisco 49ers and Pittsburgh Steelers.

I received great help from Palau Turf employees. We needed it because we had compacted soil, low water pressure for irrigation, equipment shortages, and scarce supplies of seed and fertilizer. A Guns N' Roses concert and an international track meet were held just days before the contest.

1994 World Cup

FIFA officials liked the Rose Bowl field so much, they welcomed the U.S. putting in a bid to host The 1994 World Cup but under one major condition: all the stadiums had to have grass fields.

To help the United States' bid, our crew prepared different test patches for FIFA's inspection that varied in quality, according to cost and time limitations.

We needed to show that the six artificial-turf stadiums that would have soccer matches could have grass grown on top.

Working with HOK, an American design, architecture, engineering, and urban planning firm, we used a geotextile to protect the artificial turf, then erected construction scaffolding 8 feet high over the entire playing field.

For drainage, we put a half-inch crack into the plyboard so water could go through the canvas and out to the sidelines. We then put geotextile over the crack so sand wouldn't go through.

Some of our test plots had a gravel base and sand. We would use a filter cloth, a black cloth like weed block, the way I learned at Baseball City in Florida.

We put the cloth in 15 feet deep around the field. The cloth was laid on textile so weeds wouldn't come through.

When it came time to edge the field, we couldn't pull the grass because the roots had grown through the cloth. The sod was one-half to three-quarters of an inch thick.

Chiefs owner Lamar Hunt and Chiefs executive Jack Steadman weren't just satisfied. They were amazed.

But the best part? Within three months, FIFA granted the United States the World Cup in 1994.

"No question it was a factor," Paul Stiehl, director of the World Cup, told reporter Jeff Gordon. "We had to convince FIFA it was technically possible to do it."

Lamar Hunt really wanted Arrowhead Stadium to be one of the World Cup hosts, but his field was too small.

Mr. Hunt may be gone, but his wish will come true. Kansas City will be one of the 16 hosts for the 2026 World Cup.

Some extensive work will need to be done in the north end zone to add more field area, but groundskeeper Travis Hogan, his staff and Populous, a global design firm, will get the job done. I've never seen anyone grow grass like Travis.

It's going to be so beautiful.

Sacramento, 2010

A couple of old Mountain Lions, coach Denny Green and myself, joined together in Sacramento for a United Football

League team. Denny was 61, and I was 81.

Sacramento had a beautiful practice facility, which I helped maintain. It was next to recreation fields and big, beautiful buildings. The team played its games at Sacramento State.

One of Dennis Green's assistants was Leslie Frazier, who played on the 1985 Super Bowl champion Chicago Bears and later became a long-time NFL assistant and head coach.

Doc Watson

As I mentioned before, in my 80-plus years of experience, I have had the same feelings for agronomists that managers have for umpires.

I'm just not a big fan. They are afraid to call a strike. Many seem more interested in getting paid than giving help. I prefer the landscapers and groundskeepers, ladies and gentlemen who get on their hands and knees, work the ground and get some dirt under their fingernails.

Many of these agronomists think they're too good and make critiques from their ivory towers.

Me with Dr. James Watson, a man I greatly respected.

But there are four agronomists I trusted: Dr. Bill Daniels with Purdue University, who helped us start the Sports Field Management Association; Eugene Mayer with the Scotts fertilizer company; Pamela Sherratt with Ohio State University; and Dr. James Watson with the Toro Company.

Doc Watson and I were like Sherlock Holmes and Watson – but in this case, Watson was in charge.

I became Doc Watson's assistant at the 1994 World Cup.

What a wonderful experience it was being on another big project with him. There was some trial-and-error, but that's the way we got better.

We ran the nine venues: The Rose Bowl in Pasadena, Calif.; Foxboro Stadium in Foxborough, Mass.; Soldier Field in Chicago; the Cotton Bowl in Dallas; the Silverdome in Pontiac, Mich.; Giants Stadium in East Rutherford, N.J.; the Citrus Bowl in Orlando, Fla.; Stanford Stadium in Palo Alto, Calif.; and RFK Stadium in Washington, D.C.

I had a lot of reasons to respect Doc Watson.

Maybe because he fought in World War II and received the Purple Heart for action with the 8th Air Force.

Maybe because he received his degree from Pennsylvania State University.

Maybe because he and his 25 researchers did get their fingers dirty by establishing some 50 test plots, some with underground heating cables and others in climate-controlled greenhouses, encompassing more than 10 acres of land. Today, it's called the Dr. James R. Watson Research & Development Proving Grounds.

Maybe because he believed like I did that the cheapest insurance for the ballplayers is a safe playing field.

And maybe I just liked the fact he wasn't a bullshitter.

With us having nine fields, we only could be in two places at once, so we needed good help.

And we got it. As I mentioned before, the Rose Bowl crews were tremendous.

My son Chip worked in Foxborough. Because Foxboro Stadium, Soldier Field, the Pontiac Silverdome and Giants

Stadium needed to be converted from artificial turf to grass, our work began in the spring.

We resodded all of Soldier Field. I spent many days in Chicago.

For the Silverdome and Giants Stadium, we used a tray system. It worked OK in Pontiac. Where are those trays now? In a landfill.

When we walked the field, it was like being in a greenhouse, it was so humid. Doc Watson noticed a lot of fungus. He called people, and they started spraying the field to prevent disease.

Chip had Foxboro Stadium under control. He worked with Don Follett, who's outstanding. He's now retired after working with the Washington Redskins and Baltimore Ravens.

Steve Wightman did an excellent job on the West Coast.

Among the grass sites, the Citrus Bowl in Orlando and RFK Stadium in Washington, D.C., had good fields.

The Cotton Bowl in Texas and Stanford Stadium in California had outstanding natural grass.

When I was inducted into the Kansas City Walk of Stars, Doc Watson wrote me a kind letter:

October 28, 1996

Dear George:

My sincere congratulations on your induction to the Kansas City Sports Walk of Stars – a richly deserved honor. Your Star is a tribute to your work with turfgrass for sport fields. Through your work with turfgrass, you have brought fame and honor to yourself, to your family, to the many sportsfields you have conditioned for key events, to your colleagues who manage, care for and groom the world's sportsfields and to Kansas City.

Equally important as the magic you work on sports grass is your ability to inspire to train others in your chosen profession. Especially significant are your former crew members who have gone onto careers as grounds managers of major sports facilities.

Your prowess as a turfgrass manager with a magic touch is recognized worldwide. And with good reason! You have given generously of your time, talent and counsel at the local, national and international levels.

I have admired and respected your work for many years; but, perhaps most often, when you are called upon to repair – fix an emergency situation. It is easy to grow grass when one has the materials, equipment and time. However, when one has two hours, one day or even one week to rescue a ravaged field and make it playable and presentable, it is "George" who is called in to do the job. And, the job gets done!

George, I salute you for your many accomplishments and contributions to the turfgrass industry and the world's sports fields. I am pleased, proud and honored to have had the privilege of working with you for some 40+ years and to be able to call you my friend.

Sincerely,

James R. Watson

1996 Summer Olympics

Billy Payne guilted me into working the 1996 Games in Atlanta when the sod died on the Olympic Stadium field for the Opening Ceremony.

When I told him I couldn't do the Summer Games because I had previous commitments to build the St. Louis Rams' practice fields and help prepare a stadium in Monterrey, Mexico, for an NFL game, Payne poured it on.

"Aren't you patriotic?" he asked. "Don't you want to help the United States?"

He made me feel so bad, I had to go. I thought it over, then called Arizona State and San Diego crew members to go to Mexico to get things started.

We had less than 24 hours to sod Olympic Stadium, but we pulled an all-nighter and did it.

When I arrived in Atlanta, the grass was pretty well shot. Eddie Mangan, my assistant, and the crew started working at 3 a.m. We shaved down the dead grass, rolled the remaining grass, aerated it and put down new sod. We used Tulsa, Okla., grass to get the field ready, and Eddie Woerner came from Alabama to help us out.

Israel, 1997

Working with the Jewish Federation of Greater Kansas City, I traveled to Israel to help build a baseball field. David Leichman, the kibbutz's director of education, invited me.

Thanks to the generosity of Kansas City residents, we raised $44,000 to improve the field. The Israeli field was a cornfield in the 1970s. Both the Jerusalem Post and the Catholic Key in K.C. wrote stories on my trip.

I saw the true spirit of cooperation while going to Israel to build a baseball field in Kibbutz Gezer for the Maccabiah Games in 1997. We also refurbished a combination softball/baseball field.

Founded in 1945 by Holocaust refugees from Europe, Kibbutz Gezer lay in the foothills of Tel Gezer, the site of King Soloman's ancient city. That was located beyond center field. During the 1948 Arab–Israeli War, the kibbutz was attacked and abandoned.

It was rebuilt after the war but disbanded in the 1960s. In 1974, American Jews, many from New York City,

Raking a newly built baseball field we created in Kibbutz Gezer in 1997.

re-established the community, which is 35 minutes from Jerusalem. Within three days, we had truckloads of dirt and sand – red, brown, black, coarse, fine or in between – hauled in and mixed on the spot.

Israeli officials likened our style of mixing to how a grandmother would make a cake without a recipe.

As the Catholic Key's Loretta Shea Kline noted, I was supposed to be there for a week but stayed 17 days. I changed my flight three or four times so we could get the humps and bumps off the field. I just didn't want to leave it that way.

There also was another reason. As a youth, I remembered our family struggling and Jewish people helping us. They gave us discounts on coats and shoes in the winter. This was right around the time of World War II.

I never forgot that.

One of the youths who helped pick pebbles off the field is now the assistant pitching coach for the Cincinnati Reds,

Alon Leichman. We love his family, and they visit almost every year from Israel.

Palestinians and Israelis worked on the field together. The Arabs and Jewish people then invited me to a lavish dinner. Outstanding.

Just seeing that experience taught me that sports have this amazing ability to connect people, even if they have differences.

My regret is not touring the country with Donna. Just too busy. It was kind of like when I was in Berlin in 1989 to help prepare the Olympic Stadium for an NFL game.

I noticed a lot of commotion and heard U.S. Secretary of State James Baker was in town, but I didn't pay attention. The next day I discovered the Berlin Wall came down.

My hotel was three blocks away.

14

Chip Off The Old Block

"What a Long, Strange Trip It's Been."

- Jerry Garcia, Grateful Dead

I remember vividly my son George Paul Toma III walking around in diapers at Municipal Stadium in Kansas City while I worked. When he was 3, Mickey Mantle bounced him on his knee.

Later, son Ryan was 6 months old when he attended the first of his 32 Super Bowls. CBS' Phyllis George carried him around the field.

Lucky kids.

While we walked across the infield and I held George III's hand in Charleston, West Virginia, the Triple-A affiliate of the Detroit Tigers, one of the players commented, "You walk the same, you talk the same, you look the same. He's like a chip off the old block."

Chip stuck, and has stuck, even with my son in his 60s.

"I could drive a tractor before I could ride a bicycle," Chip said. "I remember going to Kansas City Chiefs games in first, second, third grade, Kansas City Athletics games.

"I grew up around the stadium, pitching mounds and grass seed. It gets in your blood."

Andre Bruce, a hard-working kid who would become a wonderful head groundskeeper for the Kansas City Chiefs, still is one of my son's best friends. They both had afros growing up and were best man at each other's weddings.

Had it not been for Hurricane Agnes causing the Susquehanna River to flood, Chip would be flying first class when he'd come and visit. But we'll tell that story later.

From 1996 to 2000, Chip ran the show at the Super Bowl as we worked side-by-side. Those were some of the best and proudest times of my life.

Chip later worked with a consulting firm that had contracts with soccer fields in Japan and China. For six years, we also worked at spring training with the Minnesota Twins in Fort Myers.

After retiring, Chip suffered a heart attack and lost his wife, Sharon. He now travels around Pennsylvania, Florida, Kansas City and the Caribbean.

Getting Serious About The Profession

Like most teens, Chip had more interest in meeting girls and having fun than in working for me.

"Did I like (working for my dad)?" Chip said. "Not really.

"But after a while, I figured I should start learning about this more than just, 'Go and cut the practice field.' "

Chip enjoyed being around pros such as Mantle and Roger Maris of the Yankees, Athletics players Bert "Campy" Campaneris, Moe Drabowsky and Phil Roof; Detroit Lions linebacker Joe Schmidt; and Kansas City Chiefs Lenny Dawson, Otis Taylor and Jim Tyrer.

"Joe Schmidt bounced me on his knee," Chip said. "And I have a picture taken with me up on Jim Tyrer's shoulder."

And then there were the Beatles.

They came to Kansas City's Memorial Stadium on Sept. 17, 1964, seven months after they made a memorable appearance on The Ed Sullivan Show. Paul McCartney,

Ringo Starr, John Lennon and George Harrison arrived in a beer truck and dressed in our shed, which was a tin shack.

It rained, so I put down a bunch of cardboard for them to walk on. In turn, they autographed the cardboard next to their mud footprints for Chip, then 8. He also received a drumstick and guitar strings.

Eight years later, Hurricane Agnes visited Chip while he lived in Pennsylvania.

"The dike broke 50 yards from our apartment," Chip said. "We were on the second floor, but the water went up over the roof.

"A flood ruins everything. As much as I missed the Beatles' footprints and autographs, what I really missed was the Pele jersey Dad got me when he played for the New York Cosmos."

Needing a job when he finished high school, Chip turned to groundskeeping. He knew the work would be hard and his father harder.

"I was the groundskeeper's son, so I had to do it better, quicker," he said. "Now, if you work for a relative, he can do one of two things. He can put you in a desk in the corner and say, 'Don't touch anything.'

"I was on the other end of that."

Chip proved to be a quick study. By 1978, he was in charge of the Chiefs' training camp with three fields at William Jewell College in Liberty, Mo. He worked from sunup until sundown. He once built a field from scratch for $25,000.

"We had these old machines at Chiefs camp," Chip said. "They drilled the seeds in the soil, and Andre and I did two or three fields in one day."

Andre Bruce, Bill Grigsby, Scott Martin and Doug Schallenberg worked with him, and they did a hell of a job. I called them SAC, which stood for Strategic Air Command. They worked at the Truman Sports Complex as well as Royals Stadium. They also worked on the tarp crew when needed.

In Hawaii working the Pro Bowl. Front row, left to right: Me with my sons Ryan and Chip. Back row, left to right: Scott Parker, Ken Shutt, Show Ikeda and Walter Komatsubara.

By age 20, Chip worked his first big game – Minnesota vs. Oakland in Super Bowl 11 in 1977. The Raiders also played in Super Bowl XV in 1981 and Super Bowl XVIII in 1984, games he worked. He got to know Raiders owner Al Davis as well as the players.

Chip and I had endeared ourselves with Davis by working his practice fields when he moved to Los Angeles in 1982 and then back to Oakland in 1995.

One day, Chip was working on his lawn when his daughter Amanda came out and said, "Dad you have a phone call."

She was waiting for a call from one of her girlfriends.

"Can you see who it is?"

"Some guy named Al Davis wants to talk to you."

Chip said "Holy hell" and cut off the mower.

When Chip reached the phone, Al said, "I need your help

finding me a practice facility. My assistant will get with you tomorrow. We'll get you out here in two to three days."

So Chip flew to Oakland and found a school with two multi-purpose fields that he worked on for the Raiders to use for practice.

At Super Bowl XV, I had put Commissioner Pete Rozelle's name on a football on the field only to have Raiders players rub it out. Chip was jokingly offered money by the players if he'd paint "Commissioner Al Davis" instead of Rozelle. He refused.

Davis didn't like that Rozelle got most of the credit for the AFL-NFL merger and success of the league.

When Los Angeles Rams owner Carroll Rosenbloom started the process to move his team to Anaheim, Calif., in 1978, Davis wanted to move to L.A. Rozelle blocked it because he thought the team leaving Oakland – where it had 12 straight years of sellouts – would make the league look like carpetbaggers.

In response, Jim Steeg said, Davis served Rozelle papers just before he was going to start a press conference at Super Bowl XIV in January 1980.

Davis then rubbed salt in the wound a year later when his Raiders beat the Philadelphia Eagles in the big game, which meant Rozelle had to present him with the Vince Lombardi Trophy.

The jury also ruled in the Raiders' favor to move to L.A. in 1982, but they lost in their attempt to sue the league for $1.2 billion in 1995.

The Raiders felt the NFL had pushed them to move back to Oakland.

Chip saw things you just can't unsee when hanging around Raiders and soon-to-be Raiders. One of his favorites was defensive lineman John Matuszak, the first player taken in the 1973 NFL draft. Nicknamed "Tooz", the 6-foot-8, 272-pound gentle giant starred in films and competed in the World's Strongest Man competition. He always found a way to get in trouble.

Before the Raiders, "Tooz" played for the Chiefs.

"I'm sitting in Kansas City's steam room at Arrowhead Stadium when John Matuszak walks in naked," Chip said. "He played for the Chiefs in 1974 and 1975. Then here comes two beautiful girlfriends, and they're naked.

"So I say, 'Hey John, how are you?' He said, 'Good, little buddy. How are you?' Now I get up to leave, but he says, 'Buddy, sit here with me.' He then introduced the knockouts. I didn't know whether to shit or go blind.

"We're talking and carrying on a regular conversation before I finally left."

I think Chip got a little steamed up.

"Shortly thereafter, Wayne Rudy, the head trainer, comes in and asks me, 'Where's John?' I said, 'In the steam room.' Then I hear Wayne say, 'John, you can't do this. They're unauthorized personnel.' "

Another time, a woman, probably spurned, chased Tooz around the parking lot, then a nearby racetrack.

Chiefs guard Ed Budde then stopped the ruckus when he bent the woman's steering wheel.

The Chiefs traded Matuszak to the Washington Redskins, but he was released, then signed with the Raiders. He helped them win two Super Bowls. In 1987, he wrote his autobiography, *Crusin' with the Tooz.* Two years later, he died at 38 of an accidental prescription overdose. He also had cocaine in his system.

Chip shared another doozy.

"In 1977, the Raiders had a Monday night game in Kansas City, so they had a walk-through on Sunday night," he said. "John Madden is speaking, and Skip Thomas, Jack Tatum, Neal Colzie, Lester Hayes and George Atkinson were sitting on their helmets or footballs by the sidelines. I later remember picking up cigarette butts. During his talk, Madden said, 'Tatum, are you listening?' He said, 'Coach I got it down.' "

The Raiders won 37-28 on the way to an 11-3 season and another appearance in the AFC championship game.

Chip and I at the George P. Toma Wiffle Ball Field at the Hollow. It's been great to share this field with my son and the community to support The Battle Within.

Now we know why John Madden had just three rules: Be on time, pay attention, and play like hell when I tell you to.

He also said, "The fewer rules a coach has, the fewer rules there are for players to break."

Chip said pixie dust doesn't make these fields look good, a commitment to excellence does.

"We just worked our asses off," he said.

On May 10, 1989, Chip replaced me as the Chiefs' groundskeeper. His buddy Andre Bruce also was promoted.

It was a bittersweet day. As my representative, Chuck Rubin, told the Kansas City Star, "I know George is hurting about it."

When Chiefs chairman Jack Steadman wrote me a letter June 20, he said:

> I ... want to thank you for the outstanding job you have done for our organization since we moved to

Kansas City in 1963. I personally appreciate your time, effort, attention to detail and the standard of excellence you set in handling of our field operations.

With the overall management changes we have made, other changes throughout the organization were inevitable, and while I am sorry you have been affected, I am pleased, as I know you are, that Chip has been given the opportunity to follow in your footsteps, and that Andre has been given a new opportunity also. You have trained both well, and I know they will do an excellent job for our organization.

However, there is only one George Toma, and I want you to know that we'll continue to support you as consultant to the National Football League and in any other way that I may be of assistance to you.

Once again, thank you for your dedicated service to our organization and may God bless you in all of your future endeavors.

With best personal regards, I remain
Sincerely,

Jack W. Steadman
Chairman

I told Kent Pulliam of the Kansas City Star, "This has been one of the happiest days of my life that Chip and Andre got the job rather than bringing in somebody from the outside."

If there was any consolation, I still worked for the Royals. I also became very wanted and needed as a consultant, which led me to travel around the country. Also, the pay was better.

Chip worked 24 Super Bowls, The World Series and has been to Brazil, Hong Kong, Tokyo, Frankfurt, Berlin, Edinboro, London, Milan and Barcelona; but he said nothing compares to the World Cup. He worked the Foxborough, Mass. field in 1994 when the United States played host.

"When Brazil played, fans came in with samba bands and their drums and whistles," he recalled. "When Nigeria played Italy and the Nigerian bus pulled in, you felt sorry for those poor guys. They had red track suits on.

"Then here comes Italy. The players are wearing Armani suits, Rolex watches, carrying silver briefcases and smoking Marlboros.

"It's country against country. You have bragging rights for four years."

Chip also has fond memories of the minutes before the matches started.

"FIFA President Sepp Blatter shook my hand and said, 'Hey, how are you doing?' " Chip remembered. "Referees asked about the field and I said, 'Looking good.' Then, 15-20 minutes before the teams came out on the field, a guy walked out from the Italian locker room and said, 'About 10 minutes before the game, can you give the sprinklers two revolutions?' The Italians had speed and they liked water on top of the grass because they wanted to make the ball skip.

"I don't recall if I did it or not; but I was blown away by that."

Because Super Bowls tend to have neutral and less noisy crowds, the atmosphere is much different, Chip said.

"The Super Bowl is huge and has been watched by billions," he said. "But you take it up a notch when talking about the World Cup. It's a Super Bowl times 100."

Chip reminded me of one other story of how much we were respected.

Super Bowl XXX in Sun Devil Stadium. 1996. Dallas Cowboys going for their third title in four years against the Pittsburgh Steelers.

Just before the third quarter, Cowboys running Emmitt Smith walked up to us and said, "What cleats do I want to play with in the second half?"

I said "If it were me, I'd go with longer cleats but you should go to your equipment manager and ask him."

Chip remembered from the Rose Bowl that the moisture rises up when the sun goes down so longer cleats are needed.

Smith ran for two touchdowns as he made the Steelers regret not selecting him one more time in the 1990 NFL Draft. Pittsburgh had a chance to draft him with the No. 17 pick but instead traded it to Dallas, which it used to draft Smith.

Like myself, Chip has had so many wonderful experiences in his life through our profession; but he earned it.

He did the job and then some.

In 1990, we brought on a young kid with a lot of promise.

Eddie Mangan.

After being a wonderful understudy, Mangan started to create a lot of havoc that we never saw coming.

15

The Shark Gets Bitten

"I am a winner. I just didn't win today."

- Greg Norman

By 1999, Greg Norman had made a wonderful transition from professional golfer to entrepreneur.

As of this writing, Norman is worth an estimated $400 million.

After he was ranked No. 1 for 331 weeks as a professional golfer – he finished in the top three six times at The Masters without winning – Norman's business enterprises have included apparel, interior design, real estate, wine production, private equity, golf course design ... and sod.

In the small town of Avon Park, Fla., which had less than 8,000 people in 2000, the Greg Norman Turf Company spread over more than 300 acres of land.

Norman didn't just dip his toes into this endeavor, he jumped in. His company supplied four varieties of turf to licensees, distributors, stadium managers, and golf course superintendents throughout the U.S. Its licensees operated in nine states.

The 1999 World Series games in Atlanta and 2000 Olympic Games in Norman's native country of Australia used Norman's turf, called GN-1. A hybrid Bermuda grass, it was grown on a carpet-like fabric composed of synthetic and natural materials.

"It's kind of the new great thing in athletic fields," said David Barnes, general manager of the Greg Norman Turf Company. "The player has the feel of natural, but the field has the strength of artificial."

Jim Steeg, the NFL's director of special events, liked the idea of using Norman's sod because he thought crossing over with golf would help both enterprises.

Norman wanted his turf used for the Super Bowl. Eddie Mangan, the Atlanta Braves' field turf manager, used Norman's turf in the 1999 World Series.

When Norman's sod arrived three weeks before Super Bowl XXXIII in 1999, it had little brown spots called Dollar Disease.

When Don Follett, the Baltimore Ravens' groundskeeper, and I first checked out the sod, it wasn't bad, but when we returned and started to cut the sod, it looked bad. The brown parts looked like a wheat field.

The field also had low spots 2½ inches deep. Eugene Mayer, an agronomist for Scotts, took pictures.

I didn't want to use the turf, and Follett wanted West Coast Turf. But Mangan and Alan Sigwardt said Norman's turf would be OK.

As The New York Times reported, we used 250 concentrated gallons of green paint, which made 1,000 gallons when you added water. We also used 40 pounds of rye grass seed and countless jugs of biostimulants to bring it to the lush, green color.

We needed a few sprayers because the green paint ruined the spray's diaphragm pump. We had sprayed other fields, but this was the most extreme.

"In no way were we ripping the condition of the sod," I told The New York Times. "We're just saying that aesthetically, we had a problem with the sod."

When I told Norman about the grass problems, he flew in on his helicopter and inspected the sod on a Tuesday, which also happened to be media day. Norman promised to look into the situation.

"I feel bad, but nobody feels as bad about it as Greg Norman," I said. "He has pride and I have pride. It's just something that happened. Physically, it'll play good."

Privately, I was highly critical of Norman's turf, which I shared with Jim Steeg. Steeg recalled that I was brutal on the conditions of the turf.

Two years later, the NFL used Greg Norman's Turf again for Super Bowl XXXV.

To avoid the same problems, Jim sent me and Lee Keller, the fine groundskeeper I recruited from the University of Vermont, to Avon Park for four months.

"In my 35 years of Super Bowls, this is perhaps the best field we've ever had for the game," I said. "This is the Mercedes-Benz of grass."

I babysat that turf for Thanksgiving, Christmas and New Year's. I sent Lee home for the holidays.

Lee and I both rented pickup trucks, which we drove to various sod farms. Lee ended up being my chauffeur. By the time we returned the trucks, I had 300 miles on mine and Lee had 11,000 on his.

About a week before Christmas, Norman joined us where we spoke to the media. Afterward, he had a big party and invited me and Lee.

About three weeks before the Super Bowl, we drove the sod 85 miles from Avon Park to Tampa.

There, 30 workers greeted us where we installed the turf in two days.

As the Tampa Bay Times reported, after the grass was installed, it was overseeded with rye to green it up, then guarded 24 hours a day.

However, we had more problems with birds than people. Pigeons. They were pesky, they were smart, they were friendly and they loved grass seed.

At each corner of the field, a guard had a radio-controlled model car. If pigeons tried to swoop in and eat the seed, the guards sent the cars out to scare them off.

This is a technique we learned from Show Ikeda, who worked quite a few Super Bowls with us. He came all the way from Japan on his own dime. All he asked of the NFL was to put him up in a hotel.

Before that, we tried everything, including banging hammers against 55-gallon drums.

You'd think we were re-creating Alfred Hitchock's The Birds. The pigeons would arrive around 6 a.m., then about two or three varieties after that. We always had to leave someone behind for lunch because they knew when we were leaving.

We took a stuffed owl out the first day. It kept the pigeons away in San Diego and Miami. Not Tampa.

One pigeon flew down out of the sky and tried to kiss the owl. I'm not kidding! I guess the birds were getting more intelligent. Or maybe Tampa's birds were too frisky for their own good.

We did just about everything we could to make Greg Norman's field look good for Super Bowl XXXV.

In future Super Bowls, a lot more crazy things would happen.

16

Sodgate

"Ability may get you to the top,
but it takes character to keep you there."

- John Wooden

On Aug. 8, 2006, NFL club owners named Roger Goodell commissioner, the successor to Paul Tagliabue.

On Sept. 1, six days before the regular season began, Goodell took office.

NFL Director of Special Events Jim Steeg and Goodell didn't see eye-to-eye, so Steeg left before Goodell was appointed. NFL Senior Director of Events Don Renzulli was a Steeg man, and so he also left.

Eddie Mangan succeeded Chip as Super Bowl field supervisor, but I stayed on as a consultant. Eddie's supervisors would be Frank Supovitz, senior vice president of events, and Bill McConnell. That's how good Steeg was. Others continued to follow him.

My pay went from a stipend of $12,500 to a fraction of that. Donna also no longer received a Super Bowl ticket after Super Bowl LII in 2018.

My taking a pay cut really upset Mike Albino, the longtime turf manager at Ballard Sports who worked his share of Super Bowls.

"George probably was the most underpaid person in the NFL," Mike said. "It's sad. I used to tell him, 'You should pick your own number.' "

While the pay cut stung, I still enjoyed being involved with the Super Bowl and I still gave everything I had and then some.

I had mentored Eddie Mangan, first in Florida when the Kansas City Royals held spring training at Boardwalk and Baseball. "He was one of the grunts in Baseball City," Albino said.

He also worked with Chip and I on previous Super Bowls. Since 1989, he also has been senior director of field operations for the Atlanta Braves. My strong recommendation helped get him that job.

Eddie first started in the irrigation department. I thought he could be one helluva groundskeeper. I thought he was really smart. I saw him as having a strong attention to detail.

I used to praise him and complimented him to others. I was told to be wary.

As Mangan settled into his position as field supervisor, it seemed he told his superiors what to do instead of vice versa. As Albino said, Mangan also knew how to feed his bosses quite a line of B.S.

Did Mangan, myself and the groundskeepers ever meet after the season to review the previous Super Bowl? No. Did Mangan and his superior ever discuss issues with the field? I don't know.

All I can say is problems started to happen on the practice fields as well as the game fields.

I learned of the full extent of Mangan's shenanigans in Super Bowl XLI in 2007 when my dear friend Eddie Woerner, owner of Southern Turf Nurseries, came to my home in the fall of 2022. He said Mangan started working with Alan Sigwardt, the Miami Dolphins' director of grounds; Mark Paluch, salesman for Eddie Woerner's turf farm; and Jim Briggs, one of Woerner's employees.

They thought Goodell's new staff was wet behind the ears and felt they could take the NFL for a sleigh ride by replacing one sod farm with another.

However, Woerner and CBS' Katie Couric were a couple of flies in the ointment, a couple of individuals who forced Mangan, Sigwardt, Paluch, and Briggs to alter their plans and do some fast talking.

Premature Celebration

Jennings Turf Farm in Soperton, Ga., had a contract with the NFL to use its Princess 77 Bermuda grass for Super Bowl XLI. We had used their sod in Super Bowl XXXIV in 2006, and it received good reviews.

For two years, Phillip Jennings – also called the "Sodfather" – had invested $250,000 and 15,000 man-hours on seeding, fertilizing, and mowing, according to a story by CBS' Melissa McNamara.

Eddie Mangan was supposed to oversee Jennings' sod for the Super Bowl. When I called him and asked, "How is the sod?" Eddie said, "It's terrific, it's outstanding."

Jennings' sod being used for the Super Bowl was such a big deal, the Georgia governor took part in the celebration by getting on a tractor. I was there. There was a banner above the sod that read: Super Bowl Bound.

"You don't get in this league by being the best," Georgia Gov. Sonny Perdue said at the event. "You get in this league of laying down sod for the Super Bowl by being the best of the best."

Perdue would later serve as United States secretary of agriculture from 2017 to 2021. He made those comments Jan. 4, 2007.

The next day, Jan. 5, thunderstorms flooded Jennings' field.

Mangan would later say the sod was too wet despite attempts to dry it.

That's bullshit. Mangan didn't maintain the sod. If he had taken care of the sod for two years, it would've withstood the flooding. Mike Albino agreed and noted that Mangan often struggled with how much water grass did or didn't need.

Meanwhile, Mangan's team worked on another sod farm in Florida.

Eddie Woerner, who had to leave for New Orleans for a job related to Hurricane Katrina, told Paluch and his assistants that when they took care of the sod on plastic, they had to be like doctors, nurses, and aides with an intensive-care patient who needs 24-7 care.

He told them if left unattended, the grass will dry the first day. The second day, it will burn.

Now, I had wondered why Jim Briggs started to work at Eddie Woerner's farm. Why would he stop working for his dad, a really successful athletic field contractor?

When Briggs left Woerner's turf farm for the weekend and didn't irrigate the grass, it dried and burnt.

Paluch told Woerner what happened. He also showed him photos of burnt grass.

However, rhizomes – the underground plant stems that send out the shoot and root systems of a new plant – remained alive.

Paluch's guys brought the sod back by slicing, aerifying, fertilizing, and watering. From there, Alan Sigwardt's guys rolled up the sod, which he brought to Dolphin Stadium, site of Super Bowl XLI.

A Mucky Situation

Now, this is where I became an unwilling accomplice, although I had suspicions.

After we checked the center of the field to see that it was level, Mangan and Sigwardt said we weren't going to start in the center to lay down Jennings' sod. We were going to do the sidelines first.

I thought to myself, why in the hell are we doing the sidelines first? We usually do the sidelines last.

About three dozen people representing Jennings Turf Farm and Pennington Seed Company were on hand to see the sod installed. Construction people also were there.

When we started working on Jennings' sod, it fell apart like a cow shitting. Plop, plop, plop.

We were getting up to the yellow restriction line when I told Eddie Mangan, "We're not going any farther. We're not accepting this sod."

Later, I found out Eddie, Paluch, Sigwardt and Briggs were happy I said this. In this area we used six truckloads instead of what would usually take three.

At this point, I told Mangan to call up Woerner and get his sod. Mangan never did. If he did, their plan would've fallen apart like the sod.

The next day – with all the TV cameras and dozens of people attending for Jennings and Pennington – Eddie Mangan took a piece of sod and held it up and announced to the people that they had a problem with Jennings' Princess 77 and that they are now using Jennings' 419. There was a picture in a newspaper of Mangan holding the sod.

The Jan. 5 rains provided the perfect alibi. But something Eddie said caught my attention: Jennings' 419.

I said to myself, how could it be Jennings' 419 when it is Woerner's 419? I knew Woerner's Southern Turf Nurseries regularly used the special 419 sod mixture.

As we laid the sod down, I said, "Best sod I have ever seen."

Now comes the surprise arrival that probably caused more than one person agita.

Eddie Woerner, on his way back from New Orleans, came to see me and the crew. Eddie Woerner would later tell me that Mangan's team wasn't happy at his arrival. Before Woerner arrived, his brother was told by Mangan's team the sod on the field was not Eddie's.

Eddie Woerner asked me what his sod was doing here. He then goes over to Mark Paluch and talks to him about the miraculously recovered sod. After Woerner finished his animated conversation with Paluch, I never saw Paluch on the field again that week and I never saw him for many years.

As the dozens of people on the field saw this interaction, they got on their cellphones and started calling across the U.S. and talking about "stolen sod." I could hear them.

About a half hour after Paluch left, I was chatting with Alan Sigwardt when he received a call from Joe Motz asking about what was going on. After this, every day, Eddie Mangan and Bill McConnell were in Alan's office working very hard to control the narrative about the sod.

Mangan thought West Coast Turf marketing director Danielle Scardino called the media and asked if there was going to be a story on the sod.

Scardino denied this, but Mangan didn't believe her. From that point on, I believe, he held a grudge against West Coast Turf that lasted for years.

I was asked why I wasn't in Alan's office. I said I had a field to get ready that week. Mangan didn't work on the field a lot that week.

About the same time there were sod issues, Katie Couric started asking questions. After being at NBC, she reportedly left for CBS on April 6, 2006 for $15 million a year, the highest amount a journalist had been paid to that point. Her first broadcast as anchor and managing editor of the CBS Evening News with Katie Couric aired on Sept. 6.

Word circulated that Couric was getting close to running a story. Eddie Woerner said the NFL stepped in and paid him and Jennings for their sod. In return, Woerner and Jennings would help quash the story.

Jennings said his sod would be on the sidelines by the beautiful cheerleaders.

Couric interviewed Woerner. He shared his confidence with her that there would be no divots.

"I said, 'At halftime, gather all the pieces off the field, put ranch dressing on them, and I'll eat every bit that comes up.' "

During Super Bowl XLI, we had no divots despite getting a lot of rain.

As for the sidelines, I remember the black towels stuck to the sod during the game. That area was muddy.

"From the NFL, I got $100,000, and I'm sure they paid the company (Jennings) that grew it for two years," Woerner said. "I discovered Alan and Mark and Ed Mangan had pulled some shit and they wanted to keep me quiet and not expose what was happening. That's the rest of the story."

Eddie Woerner added that he didn't get paid for more than three months because "the NFL was scratching its head."

Yes, Eddie Woerner and Kate Couric had Ed Mangan and his cohorts jumping.

There also was another issue.

"(Mangan's) wife is his secretary and is supposed to take care of payroll, but some guys didn't get paid for two, three months after the Super Bowl," Albino said. "Somebody told me he didn't get paid until May."

Now, I didn't get paid for that Super Bowl for more than five months.

I was at the Minnesota Vikings' training camp and having lunch with former coach Bud Grant, scout Paul Wiggin and a Vikings attorney when I mentioned this.

The attorney told me, "You'll get a check in two to three days."

Sure enough, the check came along with an apology from Bill McConnell.

I should've asked for interest.

Fuel To The Fire

There was a ConstructionGuideEquipment.com article published after Super Bowl XLI that also ticked me off.

The article said, "Initially, the sod was coming from Georgia, but the region was getting too much rain and was lessening the quality of the playing field. So they supplemented the sod from a second farm in West Palm

Beach, Fla. (Eddie Woerner's farm), where the weather was more cooperative.

"To give the field the same consistency as felt on a brand-new pool table, the crew looked to Briggs Equipment Salesman Tony Yanes, who recommended the eight-ton Hamm HD90 roller."

"Briggs had what we were looking for," Mangan said. "We chose the Hamm to ensure we got a good, smooth surface to make everything contiguous."

The fact is, Briggs Equipment never supplied us with an eight-ton Hamm HD90 roller.

First of all, that's the same Briggs family that includes Jim Briggs.

Second, Eddie Mangan preferred a five-ton roller.

I got the eight-ton roller when I went to the Yellow Pages, looked under rollers and found a company. I then identified myself as George Toma and said we were working on the field for the Super Bowl.

The voice on the other end said, "I've got an HD90 8-ton roller. Never used. Came in from Germany."

"Great, I'll give you a purchase order," I said.

"I'm giving you this for nothing," said the voice on the phone. "When you're finished, call me, and I'll pick the roller up."

I thanked him very much.

Now you'd think the NFL also would've thanked him and sent over a dozen Super Bowl caps. It didn't.

Aftermath

After being used in Super Bowl XXXVIII in 2004, West Coast Turf wasn't used again until Super Bowl 50 in 2016. Super Bowls XLV, XLVI, XLVII and XLVIII from 2011 to 2014 were on artificial turf fields. West Coast Turf had been used for five previous Super Bowls.

After the debacle of Super Bowl XLI, I told Charley Walters of the St. Paul (Minn.) Pioneer Press, I considered retiring. However, I also told him I tried it 10 years earlier and it didn't work.

"People told me to stop and smell the roses," I told Walters. "But I said, 'What smells better than freshly cut grass?' "

The grass in Super Bowl XLI didn't quite have that fresh-cut smell. It felt different. It felt tainted.

17

Calling George Toma

"You got trouble, folks, right here in
River City, trouble with a capital 'T.' "

- Sung by Robert Preston in *The Music Man*

After Super Bowl XLI in 2007, it seemed as if I put out more fires than Smokey the Bear.

At Super Bowl XLIII in 2009, Pittsburgh Steelers executive Dan Rooney – six weeks before President Barack Obama nominated him to be ambassador to Ireland – did not like how his team's practice fields looked at the University of South Florida. Neither did Steelers coach Mike Tomlin.

Tomlin then asked, "Is George Toma in town?" He remembered me from 2006 when he was the Minnesota Vikings' defensive coordinator and I helped turn around the Vikings' practice field at Eden Prairie, Minn.

"I think he can do it," Tomlin said.

When Rooney wanted the NFL to find another facility, I told him we would have his field ready to go. Employing the F Troop – a bunch of young and greenhorn groundskeepers

– we did a lot of hard labor, but we turned it around.

Heather Nabozny and Carrie Thomas of the Detroit Tigers, Lee Keller from the University of Vermont and paint mixer Charles English from the Atlanta Falcons did a tremendous job.

The top of the sod was heavy with wet sand, caked like concrete. We needed to work it like a farmer plowing a field in a pasture.

We took brooms and rakes to loosen up the sand. We worked the sand into the turf.

Heather and Carrie ended up with blisters on their hands, but they did a helluva job.

"George, this is perfect," Tomlin said.

We reworked two fields and had them looking like pool tables.

From then until the end of the week, Rooney said, "I want to talk to George every day at the practice fields."

It was quite a difference from the early Super Bowls the Steelers were in. One time I told coach Chuck Noll there was a manhole cover near the field, and Noll said, "Just put a towel over it."

But our problems weren't over.

We arrived at practice one morning to discover a logo at midfield. It's one we definitely didn't authorize.

As we walked closer, we saw that a penis and testicles had been drawn.

Apparently, a few USF students had jumped over the fence during the night and thought they'd have some fun.

Maybe they took a class in anatomy and physiology.

An NFL official who saw the logo walked away laughing but I didn't share his humor. It was embarrassing. This added more work. Fortunately, we saw this early in the morning before Rooney and the Steelers arrived in the afternoon. By the time they arrived, we had a Steelers logo at midfield, thanks to Lee Keller, who picked up paint.

My first thoughts were: Where was security? Where was Eddie Mangan? Where was Bill McConnell, the NFL's

In Miami, I'm taking calls, directing traffic and overseeing the painting of the field leading up to kickoff of Super Bowl LIV.

director of event operations? They were supposed to be watching over the fields three weeks before the Super Bowl.

You'd think the NFL execs would learn from these experiences, but they did not.

Problems Persisted

Now, some things were out of our control.

The halftime show kept getting bigger and bigger and was a runaway train. From 2011 to 2014, Super Bowls were all on artificial turf.

The amount of foot traffic and equipment on the turf kept increasing each of the four years. It seemed like one Super Bowl tried to outdo the other.

However, when we returned to grass in 2015 for Super Bowl XLIX at Glendale, Ariz., it didn't lessen the weight put on the field. The organizers running the halftime shows kept using the same large stages and large numbers of performers on the field.

With my lovely wife Donna and son Ryan standing high above the field before kickoff of Super Bowl LI at NRG Stadium in Houston.

And it just kept on growing.

For Super Bowl XLV in 2011, we also had a big snowstorm in the Dallas area. Fitting, because Green Bay played Pittsburgh.

Super Bowl XLVI in 2012, New York Giants vs. New England Patriots, had minor issues. We had to straighten the lines and brush and clean the field. Katie Deppen, who still works for the NFL, did everything. She got on her hands and knees to check and make sure there were no problems with the seams. She was outstanding. We had a beautiful, clean field.

But Super Bowl XLVII in 2013, nicknamed the Har-Bowl because of the matchup between the John Harbaugh-coached Baltimore Ravens and the Jim Harbaugh-coached San Francisco 49ers, saw more problems. Mostly it was another case of a lack of preparation in the weeks leading up to the game.

When the Ravens and John Harbaugh arrived at the Super Bowl, they knew that the Tulane University practice field was not only worn out but just 80 yards long. Don Follett, the Ravens' groundskeeper who arrived early, told them.

Scrambling, Eddie Mangan ran around town, looking for a high school field to practice on.

Meanwhile, the 49ers, practicing at the New Orleans Saints' complex, had perfect conditions.

The teams would have to share practice fields.

Thank God, the Super Bowl coaches were brothers. Don remembers John calling Jim and the Harbaughs working out a schedule during the week where one team practiced in the morning and one practiced in the afternoon.

Now, you may not think that's a big deal, but coaches and professional athletes are all about routines. They don't like it when their routines are altered. This also affected the locker rooms.

Thank goodness for the New Orleans Saints' staff and equipment managers. You can't beat 'em. Saints equipment manager Dan Simmons went out of his way to make both the 49ers and Ravens comfortable. His dad worked for the Cardinals.

Brotherly cooperation made Super Bowl XLVII work.

But the problems we'd have in Super Bowl XLIX in 2015 and Super Bowl 50 in 2016 would lead to serious concerns about how well my successor was doing his job.

Mike Albino wasn't shy about making his feelings known. "Ed Mangan was struggling with problems he couldn't solve," Mike said. "He'd go to George and talk to George, and George would say, 'Let's see what we can do.' It was always George saving Ed's ass."

18

Hollow Words

"Leadership is solving problems. The day soldiers stop bringing you their problems is the day you have stopped leading them. They have either lost confidence that you can help or concluded you do not care. Either case is a failure of leadership."

- Colin Powell

On March 19, 2014, NFL Commissioner Roger Goodell hired Troy Vincent as NFL executive vice president of football operations.

"Troy Vincent brings a uniquely well-rounded perspective to this leadership position," Goodell said. "He knows the game inside out from the locker room to the boardroom. He has done an exceptional job growing services to our players and former players, and he is ready and eager to lead our football operations group. Troy's passion for education, personal development, and innovation will bring a new vitality and vision to our football group."

Vincent said, "We will emphasize clarity, consistency, and credibility to ensure the highest standards and best practices for our teams and fans. We will work closely with all stakeholders to preserve, innovate, and develop the game. This is about making a great game even better for our generation and future generations."

I never met Vincent and don't know what he looks like. He never talked with me.

Maybe he thought any Super Bowl issues should be communicated through Eddie Mangan. He was supposed to be running the show as head field supervisor.

What I do know is that in the first four years that Vincent was on the job, the NFL had four major issues on fields that led to a cancellation of one game, a relocation of another game and a few issues bad enough that they received major media coverage. We continued to have problems for the next six years.

Super Bowl XLIX in 2015 had problems that needed major fixes, and Super Bowl 50 in 2016 resulted in a slippery field. In addition, the 2016 Hall of Fame was canceled because of poor field conditions, and the Nov. 19, 2018, Monday night game between the Kansas City Chiefs and Los Angeles Rams was moved to L.A. from Mexico because of poor conditions.

2016 Hall Of Fame Game, Canton, Ohio

Hall of Fame President David Baker told NFL Media's Steve Wyche the field had been used for one year at the Superdome in New Orleans and passed safety tests. After the cover was removed the morning of the game, Baker said, the field also passed safety tests.

At 5:30 p.m., Baker said he was told there was a problem at midfield and in the end zones. While some of the paint was congealing, the field rubberized, which could cause players to slip. He said grounds crew members tried to alleviate that by dropping loose pellets, but after talking to the Green Bay Packers and Indianapolis Colts coaches and team personnel, they thought there may be a problem underneath the surface.

"We think we could make it playable, that it might be playable now, but if there is any concern, anything in the minds of players, we want to err on the side of player safety," Baker said. "This is the Pro Football Hall of Fame. You've heard me many, many times talk about our values of commitment, integrity, courage, respect, and excellence. If we don't have that integrity to respect our players and respect their safety, then we shouldn't be doing this job.

"It was a difficult decision to make. ... But in some respects, it was an easy, ethical decision."

What the NFL needed was a man like Baker to run the Super Bowl fields. He retired in 2021.

Vincent took the blame for the circumstances that led to the Hall of Fame Game being canceled, according to ESPN.

In a memo addressed to all 32 NFL teams, Vincent said that final responsibility for a mistake made by a third party fell on him.

"While the HOF field situation underscored the challenges in working with third parties, ultimately I am accountable for ensuring the field is of the highest standard," Vincent said.

He also made clear that the NFL's football operations department "must demand and expect an extra level of detail in adhering to NFL standards ... for non-club fields."

Seven years after the Hall of Fame Game was canceled because of poor field conditions, the NFL agreed to settle a lawsuit over the incident. According to Pro Football Talk, the league reached a settlement with ticket holders for $750,000.

Mexico City Game Moved To Los Angeles, 2018

Estadio Azteca looked pock-marked.

Players had strongly considered not playing if the league had opted to keep the game in Mexico City, sources told ESPN's Adam Schefter. Soccer matches and concerts along with a significant amount of rainfall left the field a mess.

The league, in a statement, said it consulted with the NFL Players Association – as well as club field experts and local and independent outside experts – in making the decision to move the game, as the field at Estadio Azteca did not meet NFL standards for playability and consistency.

"We have worked extensively with our partners at Estadio Azteca for months in preparation for this game," Mark Waller, NFL executive vice president of international, said in a statement. "Until very recently, we had no major concerns. But, the combination of a difficult rainy season and a heavy multi-event calendar of events at the stadium have resulted in significant damage to the field that presents unnecessary risks to player safety and makes it unsuitable to host an NFL game.

"As a result, we have determined that moving the game is the right decision, and one that we needed to announce now in order to allow our teams and fans to make alternate arrangements."

Super Bowl XLIX, February 2015

The NFL brought Alabama sod to Glendale, Ariz., for Super Bowl XLIX.

Transport cost alone was $100,000.

The sod that arrived from Alabama - and approved by Mangan - looked awful. However, problems were averted when we put an extra 20 pounds of seeds in the sod and pin-spiked them deep in the soil.

Mangan used many thousands of dollars on the best micronutrients on the market.

Charles English again was the paint mixer. At a cost of $20,000, he mixed green paint.

When Alan Sigwardt visited, he told Mangan he needed extra-bright white lines, so Mangan had our men go over the white lines. Twice.

That created a paste.

That pissed off the groundskeepers because those lines weren't going to dry for a good 24 hours. Despite workers putting towels over every line and dabbing them, the field was wet the whole game.

But Mangan remained on the job.

Super Bowl 50, February 2016

Santa Clara, Calif. Quite a milestone for the NFL, right?

West Coast Turf's sod would be used. As I mentioned, Mangan didn't like West Coast Turf.

About three weeks before Super Bowl 50, we replaced the entire natural turf, which we regularly had done going back to Super Bowl XXIX in 1995. Before the sod went down, I raked the entire field.

West Coast Turf's sod is a hybrid Bermuda 419 overseeded with perennial rye, and it was grown on plastic sheeting. Eddie Woerner's invention. Wayne Ward was the consultant for West Coast Turf for Super Bowl 50.

"We're kind of starting anew here with what we're doing," Mangan told Business Insider at the time. "We do this on each one of the natural fields. We'll strip it completely. The field has done its job all season for them and it's done well, but for the Super Bowl we always put in a new field.

"Very smooth," he added. "The 49ers have been great, the complex has been great and everything so far is on schedule. We're kind of pushing forward. ... You could play on it today once we get it down, that's how strong it is."

There were complications. Performing at the halftime show was Beyoncé. Now, it's a standard practice during rehearsals for a tarp to be put on the field in an effort to protect it as much as possible.

However, on the day before the game, Beyoncé said she didn't want a tarp on the field. She wanted the rehearsal done on the field. On the grass.

The NFL agreed to her request.

Maybe Beyoncé felt she was going to make new rules. While the NFL has reportedly paid approximately $10 million for production costs, according to Esquire and Yahoo Finance, there was a time performers weren't paid, according to Jim Steeg, who ran NFL special events for many years. Newsweek reported in 2022 that the NFL agreed to pay artists union scale, which is about $1,000 a day.

Part of the halftime show included pyrotechnics. During the

the rehearsal, the fire burned part of the field. Eddie Mangan was furious, and he shared his feelings with the league.

While Mangan may not have liked Beyoncé's antics, I believe he also caused problems.

First, he didn't put nearly enough fertilizer or micronutrients on the sod. Or bio-stimulants.

When he put seed on the grass 10 days before the Super Bowl to make it germinate, he and his crew didn't work the seed into the soil enough. As a result, the seed never took root. It only germinated on the top part of the grass.

A few days later, Levi's Stadium looked like a hayfield before the game. The germinated seed grew in between blades of grass. The appearance just made West Coast Turf look bad.

In a postgame report, CBS News said stadium workers had to pick up divots after warmups, during the game and following the halftime show. It also noted Denver's T.J. Ward slipped twice after intercepting a pass, then fumbled.

CBS sideline reporter Tracy Wolfson noted players on both teams changed their spikes. The sod was excellent, but loose chunks of the seeded grass could be seen on top of the turf during the game.

USA Today said Carolina left tackle Michael Oher – whose story was chronicled in the film The Blind Side – looked like he was on skates.

About the only guy who seemed happy was Broncos defensive end Von Miller, the game's MVP. He had 2½ sacks.

"I had to change my cleats," Miller said. "It was a great field. We came out here (Saturday), and it was fast. As the game went on, I just needed a little more support. I was able to get the detachable (spikes) and real quick change them."

Carolina coach Ron Rivera made no excuses.

"We didn't have any issues with the field," he said. "Both teams played on the same field. As far as I'm concerned, for me to be able to blame the field is kind of a cop-out. The truth of the matter is we both played on the surface. The surface was outstanding."

After the game was over, the way the field looked, we could've brought in some Holstein cows and they would've had a good old time grazing. Hell, when they shit, they would've provided Eddie Mangan with the best micronutrients. Saved him some money. Milk the cows, bring in some cookies, and the crew would've had a snack.

I'm being sarcastic here. It couldn't have been much worse.

San Francisco 49ers CEO Jed York was mad as hell when he saw the NFL's premier game on his field turn into "Holiday On Ice."

Afterwards, York and the NFL never talked to me. When the media asked me, I lied and protected Mangan and the NFL. It was the weather, bing, bing, bing. I saved Mangan and the league's asses.

However, things went on behind the scenes.

Different Set Of Rules

A number of groundskeepers asked the NFL why they were required to have a good, safe playing field during the preseason, regular season and playoffs yet they couldn't have the same thing for the Super Bowl.

An example of this is the Clegg Hammer test, which determines the hardness of the playing surface before the start of each NFL game.

In the test, a five-pound hammer in a vertical guide tube is released from a fixed height, falling through the tube and striking the surface. The test measures the stiffness of the material where it hits.

I believe Don Follett started these tests when he began working for the Baltimore Ravens in 2005. Brian Billick, the Ravens' coach, had some bad experiences with artificial turf and wanted a field-hardness test done every morning before a home game.

When Don found hard spots, he'd soften them by raking or pin-spiking the area. Often, rubber and sand would get compacted. Sometimes a nail would be needed to stir around the area.

Another thing Don said needed to be done was adding rubber specks to the field. What studies found is that between one ton and two tons of those rubber specks would leave the field when they got stuck in players' cleats.

After 5-7 years, NFL officials noticed in their research that the Ravens had the lowest injury rate in the league. They sent over Dr. Andrew McNitt, a professor of soil science at Penn State.

When McNitt asked what Don was doing and he mentioned the Clegg tests, McNitt wrote a report, which was brought up in league meetings.

In 2015, the NFL made it mandatory for all teams to do Clegg tests.

For all games, the test is supposed to have a rating under 100g. If the rating is over 100g, things such as aerifying or sanding the ground can lower the number.

Houston's Kevin Hansen said the NFL also has independent testers apart from a team's grounds crew. Heather Nabozny of the Detroit Tigers said Toro has a machine that drops a hammer every six feet on the whole field.

However, the rules seem to be different for the Super Bowl. "It's a halftime show, not a Super Bowl," groundskeepers have told me.

The field takes a beating with rehearsals, which can go on daily for one to two weeks. Eddie Mangan tried to get those times reduced, but he may be outnumbered by NFL officials who back the performers, who help ratings and increase interest of non-football fans.

Voicing Their Opinions

There was a growing number of groundskeepers who wanted Mangan fired.

A little more than two months after the Super Bowl 50 incident, ESPN reported Atlanta Braves players considered contacting the players' union to see if they could pressure their team to make improvements.

When the Braves left Turner Field for a new stadium after

the 2016 season, the players felt the playing surface wasn't being treated with the same care as in the past and that the problem areas were the uneven grass and the unpredictable area where the turf met the infield dirt.

"This is a tough infield," Los Angeles Dodgers manager Dave Roberts said in the ESPN report. "You look at Dodger Stadium versus this field, and this field, the guys talk about it around the league that it is not the best infield as far as playing."

Dodgers second baseman Chase Utley added, "The field has changed a little bit over the years. There are some tricky hops out there, but overall, I thought we played good defense."

ESPN asked Los Angeles catcher Yasmani Grandal if Dodgers players discussed the condition of the infield.

"We talked about it," Grandal said after a long pause. "Behind home plate, I felt it was very soft. But then again, it's not our home field. It all depends on how the infielders like it here. We just have to adjust to every playing field we go to and make plays."

David Gardi, the NFL's vice president of operations, came to Kansas City, sat in my living room and heard my concerns.

We went over a lot of things. I repeated that some groundskeepers wanted Eddie Mangan removed because they didn't like working with him and didn't like that he rarely listened, which led to problems with the fields.

I didn't wanted Eddie fired. After listening to me, Gardi said he would back Eddie.

After my three-hour talk with Gardi, I suggested he, Vincent or Goodell have a serious conversation with Eddie, but I'm not sure if that happened.

York Investigation

McNitt's services were needed again when York asked him to do an investigation of why the field was so slippery.

Years later, McNitt told me what I already knew. He said the grass seed was in the blades and not put in contact with the soil.

Even though I was a consultant, you'd think Troy Vincent would've approached me and other groundskeepers to find out what happened. When there's a big problem and an investigation is done, don't you go to the people who are right in the middle of it?

But Vincent didn't talk to me.

Maybe Vincent is a great administrator, but his introductory comments on wanting to have safe fields and making improvements started to ring hollow.

The NFL may not have spoken with Eddie, but I did.

I told him his colleagues were watching videos of his mistakes and laughing. I told him it also didn't help that he didn't belong to the Sports Field Management Association and didn't attend groundskeepers' meetings.

But he survived. He messed up with fields for the World Series and the Super Bowl.

On paper, I will say Mangan is the best groundskeeper I've ever seen. On paper. Others have told me Eddie knows how to command a room. He also has a physical presence.

But his performances on the field in the biggest moments are bad. In these big games, he fucked up.

He disappeared for hours at a time. Maybe it was because of NFL meetings he had to attend that he didn't tell me about. Maybe there's a lot more politics with the position than I had to deal with. I just didn't know where he was or what he was doing. He certainly wasn't on his field, working with his guys. Other groundskeepers also noticed his disappearances.

Groundskeepers also indicated to me: "It's the Eddie Mangan way, or there's no other way."

Mike Albino and Eddie Woerner said Mangan's strength is making a field look good on the outside but not so much on the inside.

"The Atlanta Braves built a brand-new stadium; he's got everything he needs," Mike Albino said. "He could have the No. 1 field in the country.

"This is what I know," Woerner said. "His fields on TV, when they were striped, it was nothing like anywhere I've seen. They looked creative and gave him credibility.

"He knows how to paint and mow and work with rollers."

Meanwhile, Troy Vincent would continue to have more problems with Super Bowl fields in the coming years.

When he wouldn't talk to me, I decided to take it to the top.

That made the situation worse.

19

Roger And Out

"In the end, we will remember not the words
of our enemies, but the silence of our friends."

- Martin Luther King, Jr.

Even though our groundskeeping team navigated a variety of problems, I had a great, great relationship with Roger Goodell.

We were very, very close for 16 years. The harshest thing he ever said to me was, "You gotta be neutral," referring to when the Kansas City Chiefs played in Super Bowl LIV in 2020.

He used to send me letters. Through the years we had some healthy dialogue corresponding via the trusty United States Post Office.

When I worked for the Minnesota Vikings and he came to town, after his meetings, Roger would come to the practice field and give me a big hug. I felt like a first-round NFL draft pick.

He took very, very good care of me.

One time, I got sick at Super Bowl LIII in Atlanta in 2019.

Lee Keller later told me he was standing about five, six feet away from me when I just collapsed to the ground. My eyes rolled back in my head.

Lee was ready to give me mouth-to-mouth resuscitation. We never would've lived that down.

When I was taken to the hospital, the nurse and doctor said I was extremely dehydrated.

From that moment on, Lee and Eddie Mangan either reminded me to drink or would give me a water bottle.

Long story short, who checked on me? Roger Goodell.

For my 90th birthday, he gave me a game ball from Super Bowl LIII with Tom Brady's name on it and all the certification papers.

He also gave me game balls with certifications when the Kansas Chiefs won Super Bowl LIV in 2020 and the Los Angeles Rams won Super Bowl LVI in 2022.

He was there for me most of the time.

I think the problem all those years was that he had a staff that didn't do the best job of giving players a safe field. When I ran my concerns through the chain of command, his staff didn't do anything about them.

So I took it all the way to the top.

His lieutenants didn't like that, and Roger didn't like it.

I sent Roger about 20 letters over the years.

Bad sod, bad decision-making, bad security, bad hires. I chewed him out a bit but also gave him some encouraging words. I told Roger he wasn't as fortunate as Pete Rozelle and Paul Tagliabue. They had good people under them.

I also criticized NFL executives Bill McConnell, Dave Gardi, Mike Kensil, Troy Vincent and Phil Bogle.

Whether it was because of the critical letters, going past the chain of command or a combination of the two, Roger almost eliminated communicating with me after Super Bowl LV in 2021.

It really bothered me. I asked his assistants what I did wrong. I asked why he didn't reach out to me.

I later was told by other people they sent letters to Roger

but he didn't respond to them, either. Especially when they brought up problems.

After not responding to me for nearly 18 months, Roger Goodell sent me a letter Nov. 22, 2022, or 59 years to the day President John F. Kennedy was assassinated.

> Dear George,
>
> Thank you for the tireless work you did for the NFL. I know you put your heart and soul into making sure our fields are in the best condition. You helped set the standard for Super Bowls and you'll be part of NFL history.
>
> I received your letters and I appreciate your efforts and constructive feedback. It's always welcome and I apologize for responding late.
>
> Rest assured, I have passed along your concerns and they have been passed along to our football operation. They, like you, are the best in the business. They'll handle whatever is needed to be done for the players.
>
> Sincerely,
>
> Roger Goodell

I had a hard time stomaching those last two lines.

This is Roger Goodell's third staff. None of his staffs matched Pete Rozelle and Paul Tagliabue's staffs and they had less people.

The continued mistakes and lack of accountability would bring attention to the field in Super Bowl LVII in 2023. And the problem was front and center for the whole world to see on television's biggest stage.

"I didn't like the way the NFL treated George," Mike Albino said. "When he became a consultant, he should have continued being paid the same. The reason is simple: He spoke with the media and he took a lot of shit – and a lot of bullets – to protect the NFL shield. When people took advantage of him, it really pissed me off."

With NFL commissioner Roger Goodell. Even though we didn't always agree on everything, he is a good man. I always have a lot to say and I greatly appreciated that he was always willing to listen – and I appreciated working for him.

20

Frustration Mounts

"We're getting there."

"Hell, it's the Super Bowl. We gotta be there. It's the biggest game there is."

- A discussion between NFL's Phil Bogle and George Toma before Super Bowl LVII.

Super Bowl 50 in 2016 was part of a stretch where we ran into field problems. After that, Super Bowls (LIII, LIV and LV) from 2019 to 2021 – despite COVID-19 in 2021 – went off pretty well.

But Super Bowl LVI in 2022 and Super Bowl LVII in 2023, oh boy. The weeks leading up to those games gave me nightmares. Afterwards, they continued.

Super Bowl LI in 2017 appeared promising.

The New England Patriots practiced at the Houston Texans' facility, which had good sod supplied by Mark Paluch.

The Atlanta Falcons also appeared from a distance to have good sod at their training facility at Rice University. However, the sod was thin, there were insufficient roots and there were irrigation problems.

It was cut 18-by-72 inches, but it wasn't thick.

Eddie Mangan is a good irrigation man – meaning he's good at installing irrigation – but he couldn't fix those problems because a pump was broken and irrigation heads were bad.

I originally thought the field should be overseeded. At first, Rice officials didn't want to do that, Eddie said. However, a couple of days later Eddie gave us the go-ahead to overseed it.

Heather Nabozny, Carrie Thomas and I put the seed down – 20 pounds per 1,000. Eddie was running the show and I thought he'd follow up, but he didn't aerify, brush, pin-spike or top-dress the seeds. As a result, no seed-to-soil contact. When we had a good rain, a lot of the seeds washed away. It was just like Super Bowl 50.

We took our rakes and tried to salvage the remaining seeds, but the grass wasn't uniform.

After the first practice, the players tore the shit out of the field. Spud Williams, our captain who worked with the Miami Dolphins, and Eddie talked with assistant Tim Collins about what could be done.

We took rakes down the center of the field and raked up the divots. Then we got on our hands and knees late at night and put green sand in those holes, sort of what you do when you have a divot after hitting a golf ball with an iron.

Everyone worked their fannies off when it was dark. We used our cellphones as flashlights while filling in divots.

When someone saw us from a distance, we looked like fireflies or lightning bugs. Bumper-to-bumper, number-to-number.

The next day, Eddie Mangan bought a lot of green sand, which helped us get by the next two practices. When the Falcons wanted us to paint their logo on a hillside next to their practice field, we did.

Here's the moral of the story – practice fields should be better than the game field. Why? Practice fields are used more.

Posing with Ed Mangan on the field at Qualcomm Stadium in San Diego during the lead up to Super Bowl XXXVII.

Sweeping The Rug

The field at U.S. Bank Stadium in Minneapolis for Super Bowl LII in 2018 was in good shape but needed some brushing. Because the weather was too cold, rehearsals couldn't be done in the parking lots. They had to be done on the field.

I remember five hours of rehearsals with tractors and wheelers for the 20 pieces of the stage as well as loudspeakers and 12 amplifiers. Because we wanted to limit foot traffic, we put four dots of paint about the size of a quarter where the loudspeakers would go.

The company that ran the halftime show for decades was led by Cap Spence, who always wore what looked like World War II leggings. About 500 people are involved in the production. Before the rehearsals started, Cap and I always gave a pep talk. We became pretty good friends.

Brooms pulled by tractors normally worked well, but hand brooms also were used. They were 4-by-8 feet, and two people would pull them.

Eddie normally is a stickler for brooms on grass or turf fields, but on this occasion, he forgot to bring hand brooms. We had two sets that were pulled by a tractor.

"Eddie, we gotta buy brooms," I said.

"Nah, we don't need them," he said in a gruff voice.

I replied, "I'm going to buy some."

Weeks before the game between the New England Patriots and Philadelphia Eagles, my son Ryan and I went to a hardware store. Brian Johnson followed us. I had hired Brian some 25 years ago. He was working at Arizona State and was an excellent painter. When we worked together, we saved many fields.

Around Super Bowl LVI in 2022, Mangan adopted Brian and paid him well. But fields they worked on usually needed a lot of work. Their specialities are as paint men.

We bought thick-fiber, 4-by-8-foot brooms, and when we went to pay, Johnson took out Eddie's credit card and got the receipt.

One of the men who helped Eddie was Ozzie Oslund with the Vikings. When we painted the bench areas and we did them wrong, Ozzie cleaned those with paint scrubbers.

We used a crew of 20 women and men, 10 on each side, who pulled the brooms across the field. They went 160 feet, sideline to sideline. When one team reached a sideline, the other would take over.

After Super Bowl prep ended, the grounds crew made a frame, attached one of the 4-by-8-foot brooms and hand painted a sign that read: George Toma's Broom.

I loved it.

Soggy Practice Fields

All this led up to Super Bowl LVI in Inglewood, Calif. The new Sofi Stadium.

I arrived in Los Angeles three weeks early.

The Rams practiced at the Rose Bowl, which looked fine.

We had West Coast Turf on the practice field at UCLA. As soon as I arrived and saw the Cincinnati Bengals' practice field wasn't ready, I told Eddie, "It needs a lot of work."

He ignored me.

A couple of days later, groundskeepers Travis Hogan and Andy Levy looked at the field and told him it needed to be rolled and top-dressed. Eddie had Johnson work on the field. Johnson is a paint man.

We hid behind a shed and waited until the Bengals' first day of practice ended. When I went on the field, I saw coach Zac Taylor and the players having a long huddle.

When the huddle broke, I went over and said, "Coach, do you have a problem?"

He said, "Yes, George, I have a big problem."

Zac Taylor told me they couldn't practice on the field because players were slipping and sliding, making it dangerous. He also didn't want to practice on UCLA's artificial turf because it's hard and hot.

"But I have to go there," he said.

So instead of focusing on X's and O's, the Bengals coach had to worry about a field that may cause his players leg problems that could slow them down against the Rams.

I couldn't find Brian Johnson, so I proceeded.

I said, "Coach, wait for two minutes." I then brought over Travis Hogan and Andy Levy.

I said, "Coach, I'm 93, and I've been in the game for 80 years. I've been around the world and fixed a lot of fields."

I then introduced Travis and said that he's the best groundskeeper I've ever seen for football. Then I introduced Andy and said he's another outstanding groundskeeper before mentioning we also had another 10 groundskeepers to offer assistance.

"Coach, tomorrow you will practice on this field and we will have this field ready for you," I said.

Johnson finally came over and said, "I'm gonna water," which was the last thing this field needed.

Andy Levy told him, "You're not doing anything."

Fuming, I said, "Brian, I'm taking over now. You can take over late Saturday when nobody is here."

By walking on our knees all over the field, we could feel the field was overwatered.

So, we dragged and brushed the field to loosen it up and let the air hit it.

The Bengals practiced as scheduled on Thursday and Friday as I had promised they would. They loved the field conditions and also used it Saturday when they had their walk-through. I also talked every day with Paul Brown's son Mike.

Afterwards, the coaches and players came over and hugged and thanked us. Twice. I said give credit to the grounds crew, not me.

I also let them paint one of the letters in Bengals, which they enjoyed.

Now the game field? No problem. As I mentioned, the So-Fi Stadium grounds crew was outstanding.

Working with Eddie, they put down the paint for the end zones, sidelines and logos, and it was so nice, you thought it was inlaid. Phil Bogle watched and took pictures the entire time.

With ongoing field problems, I knew that I had to make apologies to the Sports Field Management Association as their guest speaker in 2023.

First, I thought I'd try and reach out to someone who I thought had a lot of clout: Andy Reid.

After regularly getting his teams into the playoffs, Reid won his first Super Bowl in 2020. He'd win another in 2023 and again in 2024.

Three world titles puts a coach on a different level when it comes to respect and popularity.

The Chiefs coach also appeared on commercials where he sometimes ad-libbed, according to QB Patrick Mahomes.

Reid has delivered a few memorable lines as a pitch man. Such as, "Explain it again – with those nuggies," for a State Farm Insurance spot. And then he recreated that fabulous Snickers commercial by saying, "Hey, that's great. But who are the Chefs? Great googly moogly," as he stands next to the groundskeeper who misspelled Chiefs as Chefs while painting the end zone.

Reid also has a great reputation for being an advocate of player safety.

Philadelphia Eagles groundskeeper Tony Leonard told me he had unlimited credit to buy whatever equipment and supplies he needed to make Lincoln Financial Field player-safe when Reid coached there.

The same was true when Reid came to Kansas City. Go into head groundskeeper Travis Hogan's storage room with the Chiefs, and you'd think you were at a Sports Turf Management Association convention with every type of grass, fertilizer, tool and turf equipment you could think of.

I decided to write Reid a letter, which I took to the Chiefs' complex and hand delivered to one of his assistants. I explained Super Bowl LVI and the Bengals having problems practicing. I also shared that we had approximately a dozen problems the past 17 years in Super Bowls with practice and game fields and that I didn't want it to happen again.

I really wanted Andy Reid's advice. I remember former Miami Dolphins coach Don Shula asked me for advice. Soldier Field was a disaster with the conversion from artificial turf to grass, and the Dolphins had to play there in Week 1. Shula wanted me to call Commissioner Pete Rozelle and tell him to cancel the last exhibition game. I told Shula, "I'm just a little nitty-gritty dirt man."

Another time, former New England Patriots coach Dick MacPherson wanted me to visit to help fix the team's field, which had switched from artificial turf to natural grass. While we had two weeks before the next Patriots game, we really had a week because the University of Massachusetts had a game. We resodded, and I stayed up there for a month.

I never heard from Reid.

I later found out you had to find the right go-between to connect with him.

It's ironic. Guess whose team would be in Super Bowl LVII in 2023? Yes, Andy Reid's Kansas City Chiefs.

I really had hoped to connect with Reid. In the 2008 season, his sixth-seeded Philadelphia Eagles beat the Minnesota Vikings and New York Giants before losing to the Arizona Cardinals in the NFC championship game.

Super Bowl XLIII in 2009 is when we started having major problems on the practice fields, which were made worse by poor security.

We should've learned then.

Instead, it got worse, not better.

And as Super Bowl LVII neared, I had all these questions.

Who was checking on the sod at West Coast Turf?

Did Eddie Mangan make any trips to check on the sod in the months leading to the Super Bowl?

Did he delegate those tasks to other groundskeepers?

Did NFL executive Phil Bogle make those trips?

Who would accept the responsibility of this sod being put on the fields?

I had faith in people such as Andy Levy and Travis Hogan, but would Mangan listen to them?

Would the practice fields be done right?

Would the game field be cared for properly?

How much time would the performers spend on the field for rehearsals?

Would we avoid field problems like we had in past Super Bowls?

All these questions went through my head.

The answers would lead to one of the worst fields in not just Super Bowl history but NFL history.

21

Prelude To A Disaster

"Fight 'em until hell freezes over.
Then fight 'em on the ice!"

- Former TCU football, basketball
and baseball coach Dutch Meyer

When the Sports Field Management Association met for its convention from Jan. 16 to 19, 2023, in Salt Lake City, Utah, the speakers included NFL Players Association executive director DeMaurice Smith and myself.

Every time DeMaurice and I saw each other, he'd give me a hug and thank me for what I had done for the players. For quite a few years, both DeMaurice and Commissioner Roger Goodell gave me hugs at the Super Bowl. Back then, I was hot shit.

"A guy like George pours his heart, sweat and blood in the fields," DeMaurice Smith said. "I love the guy; he's a master of his craft. He's also one of the few authentic people."

Smith, the keynote speaker at the SFMA convention, talked about having better fields for the players. He said over the past couple of years, artificial turf fields were substandard.

When I spoke, I apologized for not getting the job done with Super Bowl LVI in 2022.

I had warned and warned and warned the NFL. Ed Mangan. Phil Bogle. Dave Gardi. Roger Goodell. If nothing else, I didn't want a repeat in Super Bowl LVII in 2023.

There were times when I wondered:

Where was the NFLPA?

Where were the NFL owners?

Where were the NFL coaches?

When DeMaurice Smith and I spoke afterwards, I asked him where these people were when there were field problems in past years.

He told me, "It's just politics."

DeMaurice Smith gave some insight into what it's like dueling the NFL and the level of confrontation needed. It's similar to the approach of former Major League Baseball Players Association executive director Donald Fehr. Fehr once said he wanted the owners to think he was so crazy he'd be willing to do anything for the players.

"The way I would explain it to the players and the league, I have to be willing to burn the house down with me in it," DeMaurice Smith said. "That's the only way to achieve some balance.

"One of the reasons I love George is he's the embodiment of a dichotomy. It's real simple. Either the league cares about having the safest field possible and how does it cultivate that and hire the best people to do that? On the flip side, they want to make the players or union fight for better fields. It's two different ways of looking at the world. George and I, we live in that former world. The obligation by the NFL should be out of duty. It shouldn't be out of accountability. I spent a lot of time fighting that. And you literally have to fight for everything."

Little did we know that we would have déjà vu all over again less than a month later for Super Bowl LVII at State Farm Stadium in Glendale, Ariz. It also would be the last time DeMaurice Smith and I would be at the big game in an official capacity.

I arrived in Arizona later than usual because of the SFMA conference, but I was getting calls that there were problems.

Bad sod. Bad decisions. My greatest nightmares were being realized. I had been making SOS calls with nobody answering. Now I know how the people on the Titanic felt.

Two companies would sod the practice fields for the Kansas City Chiefs and Philadelphia Eagles.

The Chiefs, practicing at Arizona State, would have West Coast Turf, which had its sod used for a ninth Super Bowl. Travis Hogan, the Kansas City Chiefs' director of turf management, would oversee the field with the help of Josh Lentz. They didn't want the field sodded.

The Eagles, practicing at the Arizona Cardinals' practice facility, would get Evergreen Turf. Andy Levy, the Cardinals' turf director who does a helluva job, would oversee the field.

Levy had a practice field as level as a pool table. He didn't want the field resodded, either.

In both instances, Phil Bogle, NFL director of game operations, overruled them. As a result, the Eagles didn't get the practice field they expected. There were a lot of low spots.

That was the start of a number of problems with Super Bowl LVII.

We haven't even gotten to the game field.

Four Bad Miscalculations

In my opinion, Bogle, Eddie Mangan and his main guys made four crucial mistakes.

It's customary for the field supervisor to regularly check on the turf monthly leading up to the Super Bowl.

West Coast Turf's Jay Danek and Danielle Scardino told me Eddie never went to West Coast Turf to see how it looked. As I've said many times, he didn't like West Coast Turf. Instead, I heard Bogle checked on West Coast Turf twice.

What does Phil Bogle know about turf? Not enough to know whether the turf is good or not. And the West Coast

Turf people are good; they'll do what you ask. But they need guidance, not a cursory, "Looks good to me."

If somebody like Mike Albino or Will Schnell would've checked on the sod over the months, the turf would've been in much better shape. However, Mike had no interest in working for the NFL, saying, "It's not about the NFL or money. It's about integrity."

Three to four weeks before the Super Bowl, the grounds crew and I said we needed two sandings done. We also needed a bigger roller. Travis Hogan does it differently, and the Travis Hogan way would've made a difference.

Doing those two tasks would've made the field more level.

Eddie Mangan wouldn't do it.

Instead, he had new sod put over the field. That made it look like a giant washboard, like a sea with waves where there's a lot of humps and bumps.

Technology has led to laser grading. A person drives a tractor, and the laser will show the low spots. I like to put a string around a person's leg, then go to one end of the field. At the other end of the field is another person who has a string around his or her shoe. Tighten the string up and the low spots will be made quite apparent. I also used a nasal spray bottle to show some areas with 2½-inch low spots. That's about the length of a nasal spray bottle.

Eddie didn't grasp the significance of using a cleat tester.

For years, I had used a cleat tester. I actually made one for $5 by welding three nails to a piece of metal. The cleat tester helped determine how much give there would be with the sod.

John Mascaro in Tallahassee used my design to make cleat testers that now go for $400 and $1,200.

Lee Keller, who's in charge of all the equipment on our 60-foot trailer, couldn't find one. Now one of those $5 cleat testers can be made in less than an hour. Field service director Nick Pappas said he'd have one in a week.

When the cleat tester couldn't be found, I told Eddie to call Mascaro and have cleat testers shipped for Travis

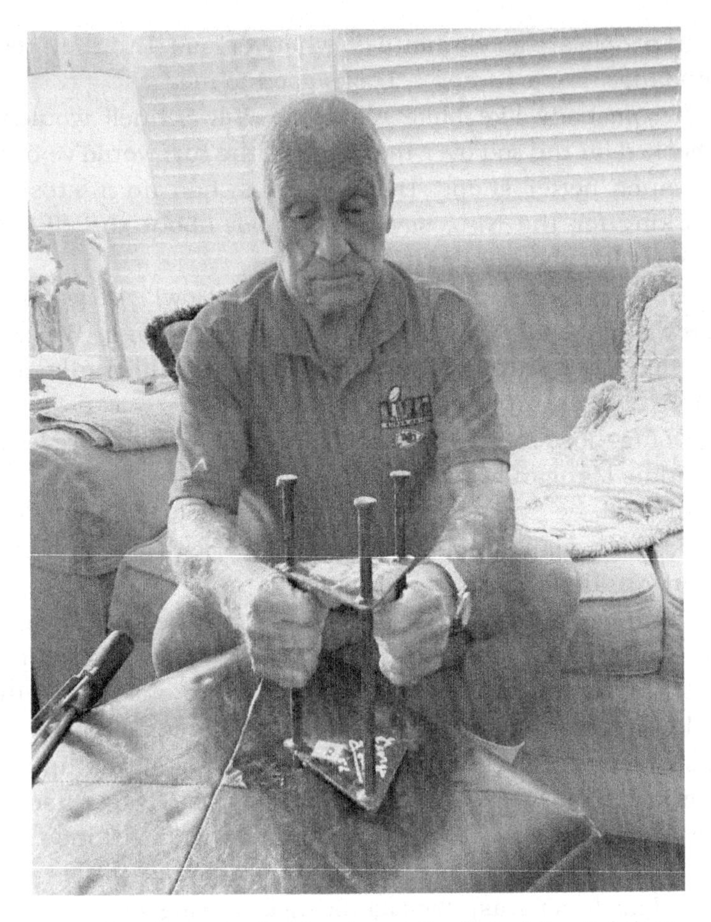

Here I'm demonstrating how to use the first-of-its-kind cleat tester that I designed to help determine the firmness of the turf and how much give there would be with the sod.

and Andy. Eddie said he wasn't going to spend $1,000 on cleat testers.

"Bullshit," I said as I started to steam up.

If Eddie had told Mascaro that it was for me, Mascaro probably would've sent it to us free of charge.

A week before the Super Bowl, still no cleat tester. I told Mangan in the morning, "If there's not a cleat tester by 1 p.m., I'm going home if you people don't give a shit."

Two hours later, the cleat tester appeared, like magic. You thought Eddie was Houdini or David Copperfield.

The cleat tester has a torque wrench. When you pull it tight, it shows how many pounds per square inch before a divot is pulled.

Our first test showed the field was in good shape.

But when we went to re-check the turf, the cleat tester had disappeared again, and we didn't re-test.

"It bothered me that in George's later years, some of the younger generation weren't paying the same attention to him," Mike Albino said. "He would call on me for additional input on big issues and I would trouble shoot for him. When I would arrive and come up with a solution, I would tell them, "George would have told you the same thing."

After a few more days of tug-of-war, the grounds crew felt powerless after talking to Mangan and Bogle. They felt they could do nothing more. They had what I called a peaceful mutiny. Many of them told Bogle that they would oversee the turf for Super Bowl LVIII the next year. They didn't want Mangan involved.

Four days before the Super Bowl, Wednesday morning, Mangan's crew watered the field outdoors on the outdoor platform or trays, then immediately brought it inside the stadium. What should've been done was that the platform/trays should've stayed out in the sun where they would've dried. Instead, they didn't get nearly enough sunlight. No good.

Mangan and his crew laid tarp and woven geotextile over the field to protect it from rehearsals for the pregame and halftime shows. Normally, this is a good strategy to protect the field. But if the field is damp or wet already, after those rehearsals, you've got problems.

When we took off the turf and geotextile, there was a 30-by-60 foot patch of grass that was mud. It was like a black stamp was imprinted on the grass.

The grass also started to die. And when a living thing dies, it rots. And when it rots, it stinks.

So Mangan and his crew had a field that not only looked bad but also smelled bad.

After saying the sod needed to be replaced, I chewed out Mangan for his sloppy approach that messed up the field. It was the safety of the players that I was most concerned about.

I then told Mangan he lied to me.

I told him he had lied to me about stealing sod at Super Bowl XLI. When he said he didn't steal the sod, I told him I heard the whole story from Eddie Woerner.

Mangan's sun-tanned face went white.

His stubbornness and lack of accountability were catching up with him. And I couldn't protect him. I wouldn't protect him anymore.

Slip And Slide

We just couldn't turn around the field. It was like a runaway train. I saw it happening the year before on the practice fields. I saw it happening in the weeks leading up to Super Bowl LVII. And I saw it happening with just hours to go.

Before the game, DeMaurice Smith had his photographer take pictures of the field. He said they were filed with the NFL Players Association field safety department but not shared with the league because of his frustration with his own players.

"I'm never going to bargain with the league without the leverage of knowing players are willing to do something," he said. "The most dangerous thing – and we'll use that turf as an example – is if you call up the league for a bargaining session and say, 'Look how bad this field was,' and the league says, 'Whatever,' and then you do nothing. They've called your bluff. And you're weaker.

"The union is a democracy. The players have to decide what they want and what they're willing to do. You also have to lead from the front. What I found thrilling and exhausting is that you're not only battling the owners but you have to pull your guys up the hill."

Throughout the game, players on both sides could be seen slipping and sliding.

I enjoyed Super Bowl LVII, my last, at State Farm Stadium in Glendale, Arizona. Surrounding me, from left to right, Sean Maclin, Zach Longnecker, Tony Leonard and Ed Harbaugh.

There's a short video with follies music in the background on YouTube showing Kansas City quarterback Patrick Mahomes slipping while scrambling, teammate Isiah Pacheco slipping after scoring a touchdown, Philadelphia kicker Jake Elliott losing his footing after a kickoff and teammates Brandon Graham and Haason Reddick stumbling during pass rushes.

I found nothing comical about it. This game was like reliving the nightmare of Super Bowl 50.

Philadelphia Eagles quarterback Jalen Hurts, who still ran for 70 yards, told the media he changed from Jordan 11 cleats to Jordan 1 cleats. A number of his teammates also switched cleats.

After the game, several players voiced their displeasure.

"I'm not gonna lie, it was the worst field I ever played on," Reddick said.

Eagles offensive lineman Jordan Mailata described the conditions as "pretty slippery," similar to "playing on a water park."

"I changed my cleats and right before the second half wore the different ones," Philadelphia tight end Dallas Goedert said after the game. "The second half, you know, the field was tearing up a little bit, but, you know, once again, we're playing on the same field as the Chiefs."

The NFL's comment?

"The State Farm Stadium field surface met the required standards for the maintenance of natural surfaces, as per NFL policy," it said the day after the game.

"The natural grass surface was tested throughout Super Bowl week and was in compliance with all mandatory NFL practices."

For more than 15 years, I took the hits for Eddie Mangan, Mark Paluch, Mike Kensil, Phil Bogle, Dave Gardi, Troy Vincent, Roger Goodell and the NFL. And I did it while sounding genuine with the media.

But with the combination of Mangan not listening to his crew and making mistake after mistake and NFL officials not taking him to task, I was building up like a volcano.

And the fact that Goodell hadn't responded to the letter I had written to him a year earlier increased the pressure.

I was ready to erupt. This was one of the five worst fields in Super Bowl history.

It already bothered me that hard-working people such as Andy Levy, Travis Hogan and Heather Nabozny, the head groundskeeper for the Detroit Tigers, were going to get criticized. It bothered me that West Coast Turf would get hammered again.

And it really bothered me that when I told Bogle that the NFL should pay to have the Arizona State field resodded after the Super Bowl, he said, "That's not my problem. It's an ASU problem."

That really ticked me off, and I let Bogle have an earful.

Levy gave the NFL a pool table, and the NFL gave Levy

a washboard.

You don't do what Bogle did. It wasn't right.

Mount Toma Erupts

When I told Bogle that the national media wanted to talk to me, he said, "Tell them to call me."

But the final straw was that Eddie Mangan didn't own up to his mistakes. Instead, he said the cause of the problem was rye grass. Dr. Yanqi Wu, a professor of grass breeding and genetics at Oklahoma State, said it was a combination of rye grass and moisture.

Now, I get a call to come on The Dan Le Batard Show; and when I came on, I erupted.

"And yes, Mr. Mangan, don't lie!" I said. "In your interviews with Phil Bogle, you lied. You blamed the rye grass for the cause of that disaster. Bullshit. I have used rye grass for 27 years, and it wasn't any problem. And those first 27 years of using rye grass, I only spent $1,000 on the field. Now we're spending $700,000 to $800,000 on the field and giving the players a horseshit field? That's bullshit. And I'm mad about it."

My earpiece fell out for most of the interview, so I just kept going for about 15 minutes. I outlined problems over the years. I blamed Troy Vincent. I blamed Roger Goodell. And I blamed Eddie Mangan.

"Eddie, you gotta be a better man. ... You're making over $100,000 a year; your wife has an attractive (NFL) salary. ... I've been doing this the last 17 years. Roger Goodell is paying me $15 to $18 an hour. Thanks Roger Goodell for giving the groundskeepers a raise. Travis Hogan is now making $18 an hour.

"I'm for the safety of the players. My grandmother taught me to help. I'd do this job for nothing. I love what I'm doing. I'll fight anybody up to you, Mr. Goodell, to give a safe playing field, and you're not doing it. Quit the bullshit."

LeBatard's staff gave me a standing ovation as I said those words.

I also told ESPN that Super Bowl LVII would be my last. "I can't take it anymore," I said, adding that I wasn't pleased with how the league had responded to field issues in the past. "Me and the league are finished. They can't tell me what to do anymore. We're done."

22

Super Streak Ends

"Sometimes letting things go is an act
of far greater power than hanging on."

- Eckhart Tolle

Super Bowl LVIII. For the first time in my life, I watched the big game from home.

My streak of attending the first 57 Super Bowls ended.

The list is dwindling. To the best of my knowledge, the only ones who have been to every Super Bowl are fans Gregory Eaton, Donald Crisman, Thomas Henschel, Harvey Rothenberg and Sylvan Schefler and photographer John Biever. John, who attended his first Super Bowl at 15, could continue that streak for quite a few years.

How was it, watching from home? It was outstanding. I enjoyed watching it.

Did I miss being there? Put it this way: I turned 95 on Feb. 2, 2024. I haven't been feeling that good. The previous year, I couldn't do too much in Super Bowl LVII. Travis Hogan, the Kansas City Chiefs' director of turf management, held my hand. The extra walking in Las Vegas

Taking in the moment with (from left to right) Nick Pappas, the NFL's new field supervisor, me and Lee Keller after the confetti fell on Super Bowl LVII at State Farm Stadium in Glendale, Arizona.

would've been too hard. It was time for somebody else to take it over.

Besides myself not being there, neither was Eddie Mangan. His concerns about his future were true. The groundskeepers peaceful mutiny led to his removal.

On the Monday before Super Bowl LVIII, sources told CBS Sportsline's Jonathan Jones that some San Francisco

49ers staffers weren't pleased with the practice field at UNLV. Because the Las Vegas Raiders are an AFC team, the Chiefs were considered the home team and got the Raiders' practice facilities. The 49ers were the visiting team.

While the surface at UNLV met all NFL, NFL Players Association and independent standards, the 49ers had an issue with the firmness of the natural grass the NFL laid over UNLV's artificial turf.

According to Jones' source, the natural grass at UNLV measured around 50g on the Clegg test that measures a field's firmness. The 49ers have a preference around 70g.

A 49ers advance group that included members of the equipment staff and grounds team traveled to Las Vegas a week before the game to check out the facilities. Despite the issue, the 49ers remained at UNLV.

That was one of Mike Albino's pet peeves. "Both practice fields should be the same," he said. "This is the Super Bowl. Money is no object. All it costs is about $80,000 to fix that field. When George did it in the early years, there wasn't a difference between the practice and game fields."

I'll say two things:

If Matt Greiner, the 49ers' director of groundskeeping, said there's a problem with the field, then there's a problem with the field. Matt is one of the best there is.

I reached out to Jonathan Jones because I wanted to make sure he wasn't getting too much grief. Jones and I talked for about 20 minutes the Friday before the Super Bowl. I mentioned to him the problems with Super Bowl fields over the years. He told me the groundskeepers were leaving the trays of sod outside for an extra day, which was wise.

I had told some other media outlets that Super Bowl LVIII would have the best turf ever. In truth, I'm still partial to Super Bowl XLI in 2007 because of all that rain in that Indianapolis Colts-Chicago Bears game. Eddie Woerner's turf held up well despite the rains. What a week that was.

I told Jonathan Jones that the Super Bowl had the potential to be as good as Super Bowl XLI.

From left to right, Kevin Meredith, me and Mike Albino showing off our rings given to Golden Rake Award winners.

At his Monday press conference, Commissioner Roger Goodell said the league had independent inspectors that found the Super Bowl field to be safe. "We had 23 experts out there," Goodell said. "We had the union out there. All of them think it's a very playable surface."

My question is, Roger, where were those 23 experts the year before?

I was very proud of the groundskeepers. I thought they did an excellent job with the field in Las Vegas. It looked like a Travis Hogan field.

Before Super Bowl LVIII, groundskeepers Pete Wozniak of Arizona State and Travis Hogan called me. During the game, Danielle Scardino of West Coast Turf, the company that supplied the turf for the Super Bowl, told me how proud she was.

"I called George, and we always talk, and I thought he'd be hurting a little," Danielle said. "We didn't publicize it much this year, but thank God it went well. That field could not have looked better. We were not pleased, we were thrilled.

"We knew it was going to go well. The whole process was great. They did test harvesting, and Nick was out there.

"The entire situation was different. Nick Pappas did a great job. A real team effort. It was night and day instead of Ed Mangan."

At halftime, I called Nick Pappas, the new field supervisor for the Super Bowl, and congratulated him. I told him his crew was outstanding. They watched the sod all year – just like we did years ago.

Pappas' appointment originally didn't sit well with some field supervisors and groundskeepers, who wanted someone more experienced. They also wanted a more democratic process.

I gave Pappas an ass chewing at Super Bowl LVII in 2023. Then I encouraged him to work closely with the groundskeepers and earn their trust.

I'd welcome mentoring him and making sure a cleat tester was on his belt every time he went on a field.

It also looked like there was some compromise on the field. While Nick wrote on Twitter that even with 40 stage and production carts and 1,000-plus people involved, rehearsals were only two hours a day for three days in a row.

Once again, it seemed as though our peaceful mutiny worked.

We made our points with the NFL execs and Super Bowl LVIII went off well.

Andy Levy said, "You have to be well spoken. If you have these kinds of halftime shows, you need to explain that this is what's going to happen to the field."

Before Super Bowl LVIII, Tony Leonard, the Philadelphia Eagles' director of grounds, said, "Nick will do an excellent job. He'll listen; he'll ask the right questions."

I can't wait until next year.

23

Toma Tales

"Once George lights a fire, he's relentless. He will not stop if he thinks something is being done wrong."

- Andy Levy, director of turf, Arizona Cardinals

For years, I wrote a regular column called "Toma Tales" in a publication called SportsField Management.

I wasn't bashful. I praised those who deserved it, and I criticized those who deserved it.

In one of my columns I wrote that Tony Leonard, the director of grounds for the Philadelphia Eagles, had been proud that his field had the trademark look of artificial turf. However, I said it wasn't his trademark. It was the trademark of a turf system that he had in the field.

I also wrote that he couldn't just take a sod cutter down the field and resod. He had to wait until the bad turf leveled off, otherwise everyone would know that he resodded over the top of the existing turf to protect that turf system.

People thought I ripped Tony. No way. I had seen Tony's work, and I admired it.

However, Tony didn't see it that way.

"I called a friend working a Super Bowl, and he happened to be next to George," Tony Leonard said. "He wrote a column that I didn't like. My friend gave the phone to him, and I let him hear my side and that I didn't appreciate the column and I would've appreciated a phone call from him.

"That's how we met. That was our first introduction.

"At the end of the day, he was right. Now and then, I get a chuckle when I read it again."

Later, when Tony saw an end zone logo that faded from red to black, his first thought was, "This started with George."

"He's the GOAT. The things he's learned, what he's done for the industry. He's right, the things he says. He's such a wealth of knowledge.

"And he's a tough SOB. He's in the trenches."

Even though I'm 5-foot-5, some people found me to be a towering influence.

Dennis Brolin, who has developed quite a business, Sports Turf Specialties, said, "I don't know his height, but on the field, he's like 6-4, 300 pounds. He's a monster."

Kevin Meredith, who had won the Toma Golden Rake Award in 2004, said when he met me in New Jersey, he felt intimidated when he had to follow me in making a speech.

Why?

"Because he's George Toma," Kevin said. "He's got so much knowledge, and his connections are unbelievable. He's been a mentor. And George is a hard-ass."

Kevin Hansen, grounds foreman at NRG Stadium in Houston, home of the Texans, added, "He's a great leader and mentor. He's always brought a fun atmosphere. We work long hours, and it can get chippy. It's a pleasure working with him."

Andy Levy said, "It means a lot to him. It's a big deal, every blade of grass.

"When someone messes up, they're getting a call."

Inspiring The Inspirational

Dave Mellor, senior director of grounds for the Boston Red Sox, has been hit by a car – twice.

I'm standing far right at the bottom of the photo without a mask along with the masked bandits after Super Bowl LV at Raymond James Stadium in Tampa in 2021. Masks were still required due to the pandemic. I love this photo because it represents all groundskeepers, the unsung heroes working in the shadow of the big game. I've had the pleasure of working with so many talented people.

The injuries caused post-traumatic stress disorder.

And believe it or not, he's allergic to grass.

But that hasn't stopped Dave from developing some of the most beautiful and elaborate baseball ballpark designs I've ever seen.

Dave had a goal of being a big-league ball player, but that ended when he went up in the air 20 feet after being hit by a car. When he landed, his leg was crushed.

"I had a lot of surgeries and time to find a passion," Dave said. "My family said, 'Find a career that you love to do.' I brainstormed what I really liked. I took care of people's lawns, I loved to be outside, and I loved baseball."

While attending college at Ohio State, Dave sent letters to every major league groundskeeper on "how to get my foot in the door."

Five groundskeepers wrote him back. I wrote a 14-page letter to him on Thanksgiving.

"It was handwritten," said Dave, who still has the letter. "Very inspirational, very encouraging, very eloquent. He said, 'Get the experience. Get an education. Never give up.' He was so supportive. He said the same things my family said.

"Mr. Toma has been so kind."

We stayed in touch. Dave visited me as an intern. He then got a job with the Milwaukee Brewers, which he had for almost 16 years. Strangely enough, while working, Dave was hit by another car when a woman drove through a gate and into the Brewers' outfield.

After that, Dave needed help for PTSD. With help from his service dog, Drago, a German shepherd, and through writing a book, he persevered.

When I retired from the Kansas City Royals, I asked if he wanted to replace me. Instead, Dave took a job with the Red Sox, and he is now the senior director of grounds. He also has worked with the Green Bay Packers, San Francisco Giants and Anaheim Angels.

While Dave has these intricate designs, I'm proud that he said, "Safety and playability are my first priority. I'd rather have a field not look nice and be safe than vice versa. After safety, everything else is a bonus."

As if Dave hasn't been through enough, he did an allergy test where doctors found out he's allergic to mowing lawns.

"My nose fills up; I sneeze and get sniffles," he said. "The doctors joked about it. With my PTSD, I needed to work."

Diversity Came Naturally

The young black teens from Kansas City schools. Their dedication? Outstanding.

I enjoyed working with blacks, Hispanics, Hawaiians. NFL executive Jim Steeg suggested women, and that worked well, too. People such as Heather Nabozny and Carrie Thomas with the Detroit Tigers have done a wonderful job. Heather still sends me kielbasa, pierogies and rye bread for Christmas.

"If you can run a rake, that's the main thing to George," Levy said.

On The Road Again

Lee Keller said his career took off after he read an article in Weeds, Trees and Turf on the Kansas City Royals' training complex in Haines City, Fla. In 1987, he wrote me a letter and I invited him down. He had been working for Chemlawn.

After that, Lee started working for Vermont's Class A baseball team. He believes it hired him mainly because of the work he did with us.

"We'd work from 7 a.m. until midnight, 1 in the morning," Lee recalled. "Half the place hadn't been built yet.

"And with George, there was not a lot of stopping to eat. If you did, you'd have to buy four or five hot dogs because it was your only chance to eat."

Lee once asked me, "When are you gonna take us to the Super Bowl?"

I told him the spring training complex never would be ready if I did that.

But Lee got his chance at Super Bowl XXXV in 2001, and he worked every one until Super Bowl LVIII in 2024 when he was recovering from a foot injury.

Lee has a bunch of stories, particularly from our adventures criss-crossing the Florida roads around Tampa and our trip to visit Greg Norman's turf farm.

Lee Keller: "So we got invited to a barbecue at Greg Norman's turf farm, and it's awesome. We were in line at the buffet, and George noticed the utensils were plastic. George says to me, 'What the fuck are we going to do with these?' Well, the steaks were so tender and good, you didn't need a knife. George likes to say I stuffed my pockets with steaks, but I didn't. Honest."

Lee: "We regularly would leave at 6 or 6:30 in the morning and not return until 8 or 9 at night. Those were the days when the NFL used to stand for No Fucking Lunch. It was a Saturday in January, and we got done early, and George wanted to drive to Baseball City. I wanted to go back and watch the NFL playoffs. As we drove to Baseball City somewhere in the middle of nowhere, George had me pull into this little strip mall. There's nothing in there but a thrift store, but we go in, and there's TVs for sale. Several were on, and they had the playoffs on. I remember Green Bay was playing. So George stands there watching the game. The owner/merchant starts asking questions about the TVs, and George doesn't respond. A short time later, George goes behind his desk, takes the merchant's chair, makes himself comfortable and continues watching the game. The guy is a little annoyed, so he goes over to me and asks, 'You think your dad is interested in one of those TVs?' I replied, 'Not once this game's over he's not.' "

The one thing I'll add to that is I did give the guy $20 before we left and thanked him.

Lee: "We're driving down a road, and George is fast asleep, his head on the window. I can see down the road forever. I'm driving 50, 55 mph, and I see something way up ahead, and it's black. And it's moving, big as a firehose. It's a snake. I'm not going to swerve, so the truck tires go right over it. Bump, bump, bump. George's head bangs off the window, and he said, 'What the fuck is that?' I said, 'I think it was a python.' He said, 'Let's go back and look at it.' We drove back, and it was gone."

Lee: "We left for the turf farm on a foggy morning, and traffic is slow going. George has to pee, so he goes in a Coke bottle. Well, he's missing, and I thought windshield wipers were on the inside. When he's done, he throws the bottle in back of the truck. When we are at the farm, we meet Ron, the farm manager. Great guy. We're standing around the back of the truck talking as we did each visit. While George's language isn't the best, Ron picks up the Coke bottle and says, 'George, you really shouldn't keep gas in a Coke bottle.' I laughed and said, 'Hey Ron, that's not gas.' Shortly after, we found out Ron also is a preacher at his church. George got back in the truck to leave and said, 'I don't know if I am going to heaven now.' "

Other Favorite Stories

Since I've spoken at length about field supervisors and groundskeepers throughout this book, I thought I'd give those guys a chance to share a few stories.

Some are confrontational, some are funny, and some are a bit embarrassing.

But that's what happens when you spend hours on end with people you consider to be like family.

> **Kevin Hansen:** "He's a firecracker. You hear of things in school and learn about him and what he did in the industry. We love each other to death, but if I did something wrong, he'd let me know."

> **Andy Levy:** "At my first Super Bowl (XXX in 1996), I had just started working with the Cardinals part time. I was a field painter. I had no idea this would be my career, but I went from a major of geology to urban horticulture. When George arrived, he whipped his shirt off, strutted around and said, 'I don't need you.' Now, I realize I'm doing the same thing. If someone messed up, they're getting a call. And if you're the new kid on the crew, he's gonna haze you. He's gonna give you hell and shit. Well, there was this one new kid, and he's going around the field with George and holding the hose for the painter, which was me. The kid walks to the other side of the field, and he turns the sprayer off. George says, 'What in the hell are you doing, son?' And when

the kid says, 'It was making a loud noise,' George yells, 'How do you know I don't like loud noises?' Holy shit. But he makes you better."

Chad Mullholland, director of grounds, Miami Marlins: "When I moved too slow on a job I did for him at Super Bowl XXX (1996), he started calling me 'Lightning' and made fun of me. Then other guys started. Now I have a lightning bolt that I put on my cap and put on all of my stuff."

Don Follett, senior director of fields, Baltimore Ravens, Washington Redskins: "The day I met him, I was at Arizona State. They sent our whole entourage to Tampa Bay where Super Bowl XXV (1991) was. We did the Super Bowl the next year. I was at the stadium when I saw an old guy mixing a pile of sand with a green dye, turning it over. I don't like to stand around, so I told him, 'Hey would you like some help?' Like he always does, he said, 'Sure, son, grab a shovel.' So we spent the day making the sand green. He then said, 'Do you want to come back tomorrow?' I said sure, so I went and got some paint clothes at a store and bought trashy shoes and a sweat suit. I spent the whole week with him. Then I worked 13 Super Bowls with him, and as he got to know me, I worked the Pro Bowl in Hawaii."

Dennis Brolin: "The first day I met George, he fired me. I was hired as an assistant at Foxboro Stadium in 1990. During construction, they had the wrong sand and the roots didn't mix. They called in the pros, George and professors from UMass and Michigan State. George came in guns blazing, like, 'My ass is on the line.' He took control. At one point, we had a slight difference of opinion. He said, 'No, do this,' and me being a young kid, 22, I said something, and he ripped me apart, told me I didn't know what I was doing. I fired right back at him. George marched off and went to my boss and said, 'That man needs to leave. I can't work with him.' He tells me, 'You're officially fired kid, don't let the door hit you in the ass.' I went to my boss, and he said, 'You're not fired, but you need to play nice.' In 1997, the Patriots went to the Super Bowl and I went with the team. At pregame warmups, there's George Toma. I said, 'Hi, George, how are you doing?' and he gave me a hug, like he forgot. He said, 'I really respect you. You stood up to me. You weren't right, but you weren't wrong.' I said, 'George, I respect the hell out of you.' Then he said, 'I want you to be part of my Super Bowl crew.' "

Now Dennis thought he was my guy, but I made him earn his stripes.

Dennis Brolin: "I walked in, thinking I was the cat's ass, and lo and behold, he gave me a rake and said, 'Go to the warning track, you haven't proven anything yet.' For a good two days, I was raking stones and cigarette butts. After those two days, he said, 'Looks like you know how to hold a rake.' I said, 'Yes, George, I know how to hold a rake.' From that point on, I put in 10 years with George on the Super Bowl crew. I can't say enough about the guy. He holds no punches. He never gave you a job he didn't do. But his sense of humor, I didn't know if he was mad or joking with you. One time he spoke to my boss on behalf of me. He said, 'Have trust in the kid. Don't hire a consultant. Have him do it.' That opened the door to me rebuilding the Patriots' field. I definitely would want to be in a foxhole with him. He'd jump on a grenade for you."

Heather Nabozny: "When we were in Arizona for the Super Bowl, we had problems with the sea gulls. He sat on the edge of the field, and every time they'd come toward the field, he'd blast this propane-fired cannon. All he needed to do was hit a button. Everyone would get so scared. It was one of those things."

Ken Mrock, head groundskeeper, Chicago Bears: "I've had Hall of Famers say, 'My legs never felt better.' You can't put a price on that. Grass needs rest and recovery. It's a living, breathing thing."

24

Are The Owners Listening?

Come senators, congressmen
Please heed the call
Don't stand in the doorway
Don't block up the hall
For he that gets hurt
Will be he who has stalled
The battle outside ragin'
Will soon shake your windows
And rattle your walls
For the times they are a-changin'

- Bob Dylan

Sept. 11, 2023.

MetLife Stadium became as electric as it ever has been.

Monday Night Football. The anniversary of 9/11.

When New York Jets quarterback Aaron Rodgers joined his teammates on the field carrying the United States flag, the home crowd raised the decibels to a new din.

Rodgers had jacked up the hopes of Jets fans to a level not seen in decades. It cost them plenty: He took a pay cut but still would receive $75 million over two seasons. New York also had to send Green Bay a second-round draft pick in 2023 and a conditional second-rounder in 2024 that would become a first-rounder if he played 65 percent of the snaps.

He joined a team that had one of the best defenses in the NFL, one of the best backfield tandems in the league, new weapons at wide receiver and an offensive coordinator Rodgers highly respected.

About the only area of concern was the offensive line.

Rodgers lasted just four plays before suffering an injury that turned MetLife into MetDeath.

Scrambling to the left when the Buffalo Bills made him adjust off what was supposed to be a quick throw – right tackle Duane Brown made a cut block – Rodgers had Leonard Floyd come from the right edge and take him down. As Rodgers tried to escape, his left foot planted into the ground, and the pressure on his already strained calf extended to his lower foot.

Rodgers hobbled as he got up, stood, looked to the Jets' sideline, then sat on the ground.

At that moment he probably knew he tore his Achilles tendon. It was almost to the day that Jets QB Vinny Testaverde suffered the same injury in 1999.

The Achilles tendon is the thick cord you can feel at the back of your ankle that attaches the calf muscle to the back of your heel. If you take your hand, start at the heel and work up, you can feel the tendon.

And when the tendon is torn, you can feel that, too. At that point, you can only pray and hope the tendon doesn't roll up. That's excruciating.

Recovery normally is four to six months but is much tougher for a 40-year-old player than it is for someone who is 30. Rodgers felt he could return if the Jets had a shot at making the playoffs, but bad quarterback play ended those thoughts.

Less than 48 hours after his injury, Rodgers posted "I shall rise yet again" on Instagram.

Shortly after his injury, new NFL Players Association executive director Lloyd Howell said NFL stadiums – including MetLife – need to change from artificial turf to natural grass. Former NFLPA executive director DeMaurice Smith said artificial turf fields weren't up to par.

"Moving all stadium fields to high-quality natural grass surfaces is the easiest decision the NFL can make," Howell said. "The players overwhelmingly prefer it, and the data is clear that grass is simply safer than artificial turf. It is an issue that has been near the top of the players' list during my team visits and one I have raised with the NFL.

"While we know there is an investment to making this change, there is a bigger cost to everyone in our business if we keep losing our best players to unnecessary injuries. It makes no sense that stadiums can flip over to superior grass surfaces when the World Cup comes or soccer clubs come to visit for exhibition games in the summer but inferior artificial surfaces are acceptable for our own players. This is worth the investment, and it simply needs to change now."

Howell's comments came after Rodgers' former teammate David Bakhtiari blamed his buddy's injury on the turf over Twitter.

"Congrats @nfl. How many more players have to get hurt on ARTIFICIAL TURF??! You care more about soccer players than us. You plan to remove all artificial turf for the World Cup coming up. So clearly it's feasible. I'm sick of this. Do better!"

Other players echoed Bakhtiari's sentiments. As Arizona's director of turf, Andy Levy, said, "It's a psychological thing about the surface. ... If they're thinking about it. ..."

NFL Commissioner Roger Goodell's response?

More research needs to be done, he told ESPN's Stephen A. Smith.

Of the 30 NFL stadiums, 17 use turf and 13 use grass. Green Bay uses a combination where synthetic fibers are woven into the traditional Kentucky bluegrass sod, according to Sports Illustrated's Joelle Harms.

With NFL teams' salary caps exceeding $250 million in 2024, players are awarded more than $8 billion in salaries every year.

When you think of the investments teams make for players such as the Kansas City Chiefs' Pat Mahomes ($450 million, 10 years) and the Cincinnati Bengals' Joe Burrow ($275 million, five years), doesn't it make sense to give them the best equipment and best field conditions?

DeMaurice Smith saw it differently.

"If you own a coal mine and are sending men down to the hole to bring back black diamonds, why wouldn't they?" he said. "The answer is, you would if the people who are going down the hole to find black diamonds are irreplaceable. But they're fungible and replaceable. When we get to labor law and leave it to the market, there's no morals in the market. So I did the best I could."

I work hard to share my opinions and knowledge to give back to fellow groundskeepers and to a career that has given me so much. | *Photo by Jeff Stead*

Fox Sports talk-show host Colin Cowherd said less than half of NFL owners want to win first. He added their top priorities are profit and control. Maybe that explains why Bill Belichick didn't get hired.

I have pounded the table for decades that the best insurance for players is a safe playing field.

It doesn't matter whether it's a grass field or artificial turf, it's about who maintains those fields.

But I'll also say this:

Before I die, I would love to speak to the NFL, NFLPA, coaches, players, groundskeepers, even the NCAA and tell them they need to work together to have the safest field possible – and then some.

If the main principals can't or won't work together, I have another suggestion: government intervention.

That would not be unheard-of, as political leaders have looked into steroids, antitrust violations, concussions, transgender athletes and the NCAA's name, image and likeness (NIL) policy that allows college athletes to be paid.

Maybe it needs to be looked at this way: Are NFL players able to do their jobs in a safe workplace? Do we need to include the involvement of the U.S. Department of Labor? Should we include OSHA – Occupational Safety and Health Administration?

If that happened, would the NFL try to block that? It does spend more than $1 million on federal government lobbying, according to an OpenSecrets' analysis of year-end lobbying disclosures.

A lot of people don't like me because George Toma tells the fucking truth. And I don't hold back on my criticisms.

Can teams constantly re-sod the field with soccer matches, concerts and other events going on? Yes. The fees charged for parking can offset that cost.

If there are 12-14 days between events, fields even can be reseeded, and that can be done for a minimal cost. Done the right way, where the seeds are soaked in water and bio-stimulants, then pin-spiked or aerified into the soil, they'll re-germinate in less than a week where the grass can be mowed.

Hell, we've proved grass not only can grow on artificial turf, it can grow on plastic. We proved that with the 1996 World Cup and an exhibition in the Superdome, New Orleans Saints vs. Green Bay Packers. The Packers wanted grass. They got grass.

Eddie Woerner has the brilliant idea of having sod or turf farms within a few miles of every NFL and major-college football stadium.

Andy Levy makes some good points.

"I think the NFL wants a perfect event," Levy said. "They want it to look perfect and play perfect and be perfect. That can and should be attainable. It's easy to say, 'Fucking halftime show.' I've been in this business long enough that a lot of people want a lot of things. If we can't deliver, then we're in the wrong business.

"It's real easy for us to blame the halftime show. These are standards that should be able to be attained."

I hope this new NFLPA leader can get the job done. He's new and will have to work through the political bullshit. He needs to have some big cojones. Like the ones on the practice field for Super Bowl XLIII in 2009.

The time for excuses and rationalizing is over.

How many of the sports' top players need to get turf injuries before enough is enough?

25

Leaving Legacies

"The deepest secret is that life is not a process of discovery, but a process of creation. You are not discovering yourself but creating yourself anew. Seek, therefore, not to find out who you are, seek to determine what you want to be."

– Neale Donald Walsch

Every now and then, I'll go to the backyard, and when I see some patchy grass, I think about what I can do to make it look better. Over the years, I've used everything from silverware to sawdust and wood chips on grass fields to liquid Downy on artificial turf fields.

With little rain and temperatures staying in the 90s for most of the summer of 2023, it was tough on the Kansas City yards. Reminds me of the Brown Summer of '58 when the outfield at Municipal Stadium looked like a huge piece of burnt toast.

It's also been tough on the George P. Toma Wiffle Ball Field at the Hollow.

I noticed some patchy grass in foul territory.

What can I do?

I've enjoyed problem-solving while working on this field for the last four years. It's been for a wonderful cause.

The land belongs to Joe Ungashick, a retired CEO who is very involved in the community.

Joe always grew up around a ball field. When he bought a home on the corner of 52nd Street and Wornall Road near Loose Park, he put bases out so the Countryside neighborhood boys could play wiffle ball.

After I worked on the field and put in the pitching mound, people around Kansas City donated materials, so it's a true ballpark with outfield fences, a scoreboard and bench areas. Brad Schrock, who helped design minor and major league ballparks for HOK, a global design, architecture, engineering and planning firm, designed the George P. Toma field on the back of a napkin.

It's the gem of KC Wiffle, which Joe put together with pastor Dan Deeble of Heartland Community Church. A total of 24 teams play doubleheaders during the week around the city's six wiffle ball parks.

"It's a wonderful thing," Joe said. "Two games on Friday with fellowship and barbecue in between.

"Dayton Moore, former president of the Kansas City Royals, said this is a little bit of Cooperstown, a little bit of Field of Dreams."

This field has helped raise more than $1.5 million for an organization now called The Battle Within.

Through The Battle Within, a five-day group therapy program has been created. It was developed to help veterans and first responders suffering from post traumatic stress disorder understand what they've endured in serving others.

PTSD is real. According to various reports, 17 to 22 veterans commit suicide a day. That's about 500 to 650 a month and 6,000 to 8,000 a year.

Executive Director Justin Hoover, who suffered a traumatic brain injury, hearing loss, shrapnel in his hand and a hip injury, said his mom and others noticed he had

As a veteran of the Korean War, I've always worked hard to support The Battle Within to help veterans who need a little more assistance.

changed when he returned from Iraq in 2005.

"I was hyper-vigilant and quicker to anger," he said. "When you come home, nobody tells you what to expect. I was resistant to treatment for a variety of reasons.

"My wife convinced me to get help. I needed to take ownership of my path and become the person I wanted to be."

The five-day program The Battle Within offers has aided more than 1,000 veterans.

Besides conversations with certified therapists and counselors as well as fellow veterans, treatment includes equine training. Horses will walk away from the veterans and first responders when they're not being forthcoming. However, the horses will put their heads on the veterans' and first responders' shoulders when they become vulnerable and start crying.

In other words, the horses know when the veterans and first responders are bullshitting and when they're not.

"In their darkest moments, it can be very powerful when they finally share their trauma," Justin said. "They've held on to childhood issues – neglect, physical abuse, sexual abuse – and you find out why they go into the military: to protect and make sure that doesn't happen to others.

"We've had a lot of people come up and say, 'You saved my life.' We see it as we created a space to be your authentic true self. Being in the military or a first responder is some of the hardest work you can do. Opening up, taking ownership and seeing growth is powerful as the men and women seek to be better husbands, wives and parents."

The sponsors' $3,500 donations cover the cost of a five-day program. It can have a dramatic effect. I've had men in business suits come up to me, veterans, and they tell me this field has helped save their lives.

When Mitch Wheeler, director of development, contacted me, he asked if I would lend my name to the organization. I had known Mitch from his time working with the Kansas City Chiefs in promotions.

"We thought, 'How do we make this field better?' " Mitch said. "I thought of George. We had an event in June, so I called him in April after spring training. I said, 'We got this thing going on, would you come to the event?'

"George being George, he said, 'Can I come see the field?' A couple of days later, Donna drove him over because he said, 'We gotta fix this.' "

After being in the Army for two years and serving alongside soldiers from Turkey and France, I wanted to actively contribute to making the field look good. So I went over in my red pickup and started working on it. After Super Bowl LVI in 2022, I brought back a piece of sod from a practice field. It took. I also sent Joe Ungashick a piece of sod.

"I arrive home, and there's this FedEx box and it's heavy," Joe said. "George cut out a piece of the Super Bowl turf and sent it to me two weeks before the game. He said, 'You'll want this as a centerpiece for your Super Bowl party.'

Players young and old try to hit a homer at the George P. Toma Wiffle Ball Field at the Hollow.

"And it's January, so I had to take care of it so it continued to grow."

I think I surprised Mitch and the gang. On one hand, they were elated to have me lend my services. On the other hand, they couldn't afford to pay me.

They didn't need to. I believed in the cause. The field is a combination of the Green Monster in Boston, Wrigley Field in Chicago and Tiger Stadium and Comerica Park in Detroit with a brown strip from the pitcher's mound to home plate.

I spent many, many hours on the field so it would be hardy and games could be played from 8 a.m. to 8 p.m. This helped a lot of those charitable games avoid being postponed.

Among the people I worked on the field with were Marty Siler, owner of Epic Landscape Productions, and his son Luke. Marty had a 1969 Kansas City Chiefs football, which he had me sign. I knew Marty's father, Frank, who was a landscape contractor and turf farmer.

Marty, who worked at Walt Disney World, looked at me as

a true pioneer of groundskeeping with all the different places in the world that I worked. He compared me to Lewis and Clark – Captain Meriwether Lewis and Second Lt. William Clark. Lewis and Clark met with 10 members in St. Charles, Mo., before going up the Missouri River. They explored the western portion of the country after the Louisiana Purchase, which included 530 million acres of land bought from France in 1803 for $15 million. The purchase included land from 15 U.S. states and two Canadian provinces.

For those people who volunteered to work on the field, I liked to bring footballs Tom Brady and Patrick Mahomes threw in the Super Bowl and then let them toss them around. Thank you, Roger Goodell.

I also brought back some confetti and towels from the benches. I don't think anybody missed them. Kids ages 6-13 also helped paint the field. Mitch said when turf companies, dirt companies and other sponsors heard I was involved, they also donated. That warmed my heart.

"I tried to say George's name as soon as possible because it's the ultimate gold card," he said. "They'd say, 'Did you say George Toma?' Next thing you know, we were getting seed or fertilizer or turf or lighting."

Mitch added when "the best groundskeeper in the world is working on your field, it also adds to the experience. It's also why people are willing to pay $3,500."

I don't think about my legacy a lot, but I am proud of being associated with The Battle Within.

I'm also proud that I brought attention and recognition to my profession.

I "adopted" and mentored a lot of groundskeepers, and whenever possible, I either promoted from within or I'd recommend them for higher-paying jobs elsewhere.

Groundskeepers often were overlooked in my early years. Once a team's season ended, the groundskeepers had to find work elsewhere, even though they had worked nights, weekends and holidays and often toiled 60, 70, 80 hours a week.

Standing at home plate with Mitch Wheeler of The Battle Within at the George P. Toma Wiffle Ball Field at the Hollow.

Now, groundskeepers are getting vacation time after their seasons end.

Those who oversee the fields for pro teams are making six-figure salaries.

Men such as my son Chip and Miami Marlins groundskeeper Chad Mullholland have spoken and been consultants around the world. Chad also is selling the same style of nail boards I did and has built a business on a website.

"I could've never imagined all this," Chad said. "George always kept in contact, showed interest in me and gave me that boost."

I heard a story Florida Gulf Coast University coach Dave Tollett told about a field he started from scratch when the school began playing baseball on campus in 2004. I was recruited by Duane Swanson, a huge sponsor of the program. The stadium is now called Swanson Stadium. The field I helped develop became ranked as one of the top 20 in the country.

Many of those black youths I worked with on grounds crews are now in their 70s. I still get calls from them from all over the country. Men such as Nelson Thomas want to start a foundation in my name and give scholarships so black youths can become groundskeepers or learn a trade.

All this makes me feel really good.

I'm Hanging In There

At 95, I'm hanging in there. The doctors are amazed that I have no arthritis in my knees. Must've been all that walking. I still have those Popeye calves Chad remembers from me working and walking backwards. On my hands are thick calluses. Someone once described my skin as smooth but completely inflexible, like hardened plastic.

Despite regularly taking off my shirt and rarely putting on sun-tan lotion while I worked, my wrinkled upper-body armor hasn't been hit by skin cancer. There are some small light spots that get burned off yearly.

Age is catching up to me. When I went to the Kansas City Royals Hall of Fame and wore my royal blue jacket with pride, my good friend Freddie Patek and I had to attend in wheelchairs. I also have to use a cane when I walk.

When people ask how I'm doing, I say I'm hanging in there. But mentally, I hurt at times. I still agonize over the way my relationship ended with Roger and the NFL. I'm not angry, and when I do eat, it's often Chester's Puffcorn. Not the best. Tastes good, though.

DeMaurice Smith said Roger's responses and non-responses are basically saying the NFL is going to do what the NFL wants to do and I can't take it so personally.

"Roger Goodell is one of the most confrontational people outside of me," DeMaurice said. "We look for language that's very confrontational. We look for language that shows some type of emotion. The league uses language that is utterly confrontational."

DeMaurice Smith said it's his wish that I focus on all the wonderful things I've done.

"He's had a tremendous career," DeMaurice said. "(George) should not let any of this corrupt what he's done.

"You can't let the NFL suck the joy out of you, because they suck the joy out of a clown. They're awful."

Sometimes, I think my words are falling on deaf ears.

Then I received this letter on Aug. 31, 2023, from Mike Andresen, a long-time ally who now is a retired groundskeeper who worked at Iowa State and Kirkwood Community College. He's also been on the board of directors for the Sports Field Management Association.

He wrote:

> Hi George,
>
> I hope this note finds you and all of your family well and in good health.
>
> As football season gets set to begin, and just around the corner is the best part of baseball season. You have been on my mind every day.
>
> I am reminded of your impact on our profession and the sports we take care of. You stood up for safe fields when others did not or could not. Your advocacy for safer fields have benefited millions of young athletes throughout the world and helped launch thousands of great careers for men and women like me.
>
> Thank you for that and thank you for your friendship. Looking forward to our paths crossing again soon.
>
> Sincerely,
>
> Mike Andresen

The timing of the letter couldn't have been better. It reminded me of the kind words Bob Woolford, who worked at Shawnee Mission Medical Center, made after he observed how hard my crew and I toiled. He gave me the phrase I use so often, "They did the job – and then some."

Bob passed in 2022.

I'm not bitter. I'm Catholic. I don't hate anyone. It's like a line in the prayer "Our Father": And forgive us our trespasses, as we forgive those who trespass against us.

I still love Roger very much. When he came to Kansas City for the 2023 NFL regular-season opener, I would've loved to have shaken his hand, then grabbed him and taken him down to field level.

I would've wanted him to touch the grass, then lay down on a perfectly manicured and level playing field that the Chiefs' Travis Hogan and his staff created. It was like a pool table. Not a vegetable farm or mammoth washboard, like Super Bowl LVII that February.

Then I would've liked to have him turn around and look in every direction and see what the standard is for an NFL quality field.

Ah, we can dream.

For the first time in 80 years, I have been home regularly. Donna has been so good, taking me to doctors. I hope she can put up with me. When a problem gnaws at me, I can chew on it like a dog does a bone.

It is a new era for groundskeepers. There's a lot of good ones out there. A lot of and-then-some type of guys and gals.

When I watched the Chiefs-Dolphins game in Frankfurt, Germany, the first thing I saw was the most green and beautiful grass playing field.

As you all know, I am for outstanding-looking and safe fields. Every game I watch, I concentrate on the playing field: How does it hold up after all the plays during NFL and college games?

I find that the majority of them are in excellent shape. Yes, that includes high school fields.

But the field the NFL used in Frankfurt hit me hard. I hadn't seen such a beautiful, safe field like this in years. If we were giving out game balls, this field and grounds crew would get one, both Americans and Germans.

This would get my vote for best field of the year. Whoever was in charge and everyone who helped should get a sincere thank-you.

Acknowledgments

"I've learned that people will forget what you said, people will forget what you did, but people will never forget how you made them feel."

- Dr. Maya Angelou

I've met a lot of people throughout my eight-decade career, and there's a long list of folks I want to thank.

Before we get to those whom I worked with and built strong relationships and friendships with, I want to start by thanking my entire family. Family members are the ones who sacrificed. They're the ones who saw my faults and quirks and yet they still love me.

To my wife Donna. She blessed me with my son Ryan. We have lived a life based around sports but have traveled to many places – Hawaii, Japan, Germany, Spain, Mexico, and Israel. She also has scheduled appointments and taken me to see doctors for my health issues. I appreciate that, although I don't say it as much as I should.

To my sons Chip and Ryan, an international Delta pilot, who have worked side-by-side with me and escorted me to various sports stadiums over the years. To my son Rick, a lieutenant and tank commander in Desert Storm, who now is a COO of a financial company. They all have been successes in my eyes and have overcome various adversities ... and then some. They have given Donna and I seven grandchildren and eight great-grandchildren. Many call me pop pop. Now, they're also making a contribution to society. I'm very proud.

My three sons. Above from left to right, Rick, me and Chip at the Luzerne County Sports Hall of Fame. Below is Ryan hard at work. What else would you expect from the Tomas!

To my parents, Mary and George, who instilled great values and a strong work ethic in me.

To my sister Catherine, who lived to 96. She was married to Stanley Dulski, a hard-working man, and they had two daughters, Suzanne and Dorothy, along with a grandson, Jeffrey. Suz married Ed Dicton. You couldn't ask for a better husband. Dorothy married Norman Zimmerman, who passed away. The girls took very good care of their mother until she passed.

Thank you to Grandma Toma, Grandma Noosh, Aunt Eva, Uncle Jay Yarrish, John Noosh and the Washko family, as well as Aunt Anna Clem, Aunt Mary Prezlock and cousin Valerie Fleming. I always enjoyed coming home to wonderful Slavic food.

Thank you to my first wife, Helen Hornyak, who blessed me with Chip and Rick.

Thank you to childhood friends John Zielen; his wife, Marie; his brothers; Stanley, Edward and Frank; as well as Dick Kotch, Ed O'Britis and Ralph Sternick.

Also, a shout-out to Tom Jenkins. Our clubhouse was his basement.

Thank you to the nurses and doctors who were there when I needed them.

In 1973, I could've lost my sight. After a match at Arrowhead Stadium between the North American Soccer League all-stars, and the Soviet champions, we were washing the soccer lines off the field. We were tired, so we came back the next morning. We left ammonia in a tank, and it ate the pump.

Normally when I'm pressing the pump, I hold it out to the side. This time, I was looking down the sidelines while pumping. The pump ruptured and hit me right in the eyes. Quickly, Bobby Yarborough, the team equipment manager and assistant trainer, rushed me into the office, where my eyes were flushed with cold water before ice packs were applied.

We then saw Dr. Becker, the Chiefs' eye doctor, who met Donna and I in the parking lot. He took good care of me, as did Dr. Miranda Bishara. That ammonia can eat the skin off your hands, so imagine what it can do to your eyes. For a while, I couldn't see out of my right eye. Scared that I may go blind, I had my eyes bandaged. I should've stayed at home, but I couldn't. I just couldn't. Donna drove me to work.

Also, my sincere gratitude to Dr. Borkon, who did my heart valve. The dear man still keeps in touch with me. Dr. Mertz and Dr. Austenfeld, who retired, also took good care of me for years and years.

I had a serious health scare with a blood clot in 2013. It was the same year that I received an aortic valve replacement that almost killed me. I spent seven weeks in the hospital. Donna took great care of me and brought me three meals a day because I wouldn't eat the hospital food.

Thanks to those who helped me in 1983 when I broke my collarbone. A bolt broke loose from the three-wheeler I was driving, and it threw me into a tree at the Truman Sports Complex, across the street from Royals Stadium.

Another time when I fainted because of dehydration while at the Minnesota Twins' spring training complex, the EMTs took me to the hospital. "I don't like you driving across the grass," I said while being treated. Kind of funny. Kind of. Not my best moment.

Thanks to people representing different organizations:

To the media – people such as Bobby Patton, Bill O'Boyle, Joe McGuff and Dick Kaegel followed my exploits as well as reporters with the Kansas City newspapers and TV stations.

To Alan Goforth, who wrote my first book, *Nitty Gritty Dirt Man.*

The Battle Within is a cause dear to my heart. Thanks to Joe Ungashick, Justin Hoover, Mitch Wheeler, his dad and other volunteers such as Marty Siler and his late dad, Frank, a great turf man who I once worked with. Also, thanks to Frank Masterson, Rex Hudler, Josh Krasovec and his wife. Frank, the director of operations at Midwest Laser Leveling, brought his big equipment to the George P. Toma Wiffle Ball Field. He also used that equipment on the Kansas City Current women's soccer field, which opened in spring 2024 with its Bermuda turf. I'm so proud of him.

To my good friend Ollie Leyva. I could not pass up this opportunity to express to you and your crew my very sincerest thank-you and appreciation in working with you at the George P. Toma Wiffle Ball Field at Uncle Joe Ungashick's mansion as we helped The Battle Within. You also worked on my yard. When Mitch Wheeler asked me to help him out with the field the first year, we had a lot of work to do in order to get it ready for the Wiffle Ball League and The Battle Within games. I needed to have excellent help, so I became a scout. I asked Uncle Joe if I could use you, and he said yes, so you and I started to work as a team. As we worked on the grass, the dirt and the sliding pits, we got the field in excellent shape. For Year 2, we started receiving donations from so many people. Anything we needed, people donated. Jeremy Tate's Turf donated the artificial turf. It rivaled the surface at Royals Stadium. We got the job done for Years 3 and 4, although you had to fight to get the grass back each spring for good ol' Uncle Joe, who let the kids play on the field in the fall and winter.

If you drive by, you would see a sea of red with all the kids thinking they are Kansas City Chiefs. In my fourth year, my health issues hit me hard, so Ollie took over. He was always there. As I look back on the management of this field, I look at the work. The first three letters in management are M-A-N – and

Signing a few autographs. I get new fans every day at the George P. Toma Wiffle Ball Field at the Hollow and I just love it. Being able to pass along the love of sports to kids is simply the best feeling for me.

Ollie, you are the man who always did the job. I enjoyed seeing your oldest son, Wyatt, a sophomore in high school, paint the lines on the artificial turf as if they were inlaid. Yes, my friends in Los Angeles at Sofi Stadium would be so proud of him, and that's saying something because that L.A. crew is the best in the world. I also enjoyed Jonathan Leyva following me around. Once again, Ollie, thank you for all the nice things that you have done for me. I appreciate all the thoughtfulness, which is such a big part of you. I did adopt your crew. Ollie, may God bless you and your crew.

Also thanks again Mitch and Uncle Joe. You made my years at the Wiffle Ball Field happy ones. These people were there for me when I needed them.

To Dale Getz and Boyd Montgomery with the Toro Company. They also supplied brooms so the field could be brushed in that cold, cold weather.

Thank you to the Kansas City Royals players – past and present – who came to the George P. Toma Wiffle Ball Field at the Hollow for dedication ceremonies. When you showed up during COVID, that meant a lot to me.

Thanks Bob Terry for putting up my name on the George P. Toma Wiffle Ball Field at the Hollow.

Top of the morning to professor Mike Ward, president of the George P. Toma Breakfast Club. Members include Clyde North, a great handball player; vice president Joseph Dragosh; former New York Yankees and Brooklyn/L.A. Dodgers pitcher and baseball historian Fred Kipp; plus the people of Village Inn in Mission, Kansas.

A sincere and then some thank you to Jim Carnes, owner of International Seeds who helped me in the 1960s at the old Kansas City Municipal Stadium all the way to Super Bowls, plus his lovely wife, Dorothea. Also thanks to Harry Stalford, Doug Toews and Rich Underwood along with Derby, Gator and Regal seed.

Thanks to Olympic organizers Peter Ueberroth and Billy Payne for trusting me to work at the Summer Games. Rich Gonzales and Will Schnell helped us keep the Rose Bowl looking pretty.

Thank you Doug Schattinger, president of Pioneer Athletic, whose paint we used on the football fields. So many kind deeds he did for me.

Also, thanks to Jeff Logan, head of the Kansas City Historical Society, and Dave Starbuck.

Thank you to Municipal Stadium, my favorite venue. So many events, so many memories:

Thank you, Wolfpack. The zoo. The Beatles. Billy Graham's crusade.

Chasing Lamar Hunt off the field. His beautiful wife Norma.

Turning that stadium from baseball to football.

Thanks to another great stadium I worked at: the Orange Bowl, especially in the early days.

I remember head groundskeeper Dale Sandin coming to help with a tie and white shirt. He told me he had to be professional when painting. Then plop,

plop, some paint got on him, and he looked like a Christmas tree. "Now you're a professional," I said. Stadium manager Al Rubio also shined. At Joe Robbie Stadium, I also remember Edwin Lamour, Tim Collins, Spud Williams, Sergio Canales, Ken Schilling and Alan Sigwardt.

Special thanks to Tom Wilson and his wife for taking me to doctor appointments while I worked at the Super Bowl.

I worked with a lot of teams, and there are some individuals I'd like to thank:

To my Royals co-workers: Al Zych and Mike Burkhalter, the equipment managers; Trevor Vance and Johnnie Reed; Cedric Tallis, the first general manager; trainer Mickey Cobb; trainers Paul McGannon, Billy Jones, and Nick Schwartz; and three outstanding women – Nancy Gaba, Chris Rice, and Connie Leonard. They had my back. So did Bob Frank and Jay Hinrichs.

I'd like to thank the Hunt family as well as one of the best groundskeepers, Chip Toma, and his staff of Doug Schallenberg, Andre Bruce, Scotty Martin, Gary Wilkes, his brothers and the rest of the crew. In 1996, Gary Wilkes painted all the Olympic logos in Atlanta for the Summer Games. He's an artist and good groundskeeper.

The Chicago Bears and former coach Mike Ditka as well as Tim LeFevour, John Nolan, Ken Mrock, Jim Dugan and crew.

The Minnesota Vikings with outstanding owners Zygi and Mark Wilf, coaches, front office, training and equipment staff plus turf manager Grant Davisson. I also remember Ben Theis, a great worker and No. 1 fan. At each game, Ben wore his painted Vikings face and Vikings game outfit. Also, Steve Poppen and Mary Redmond.

Coach Kevin Stefanski of the Cleveland Browns. He deserved to be coach of the year after the 2023 season with all those quarterback injuries. The Browns also made the playoffs.

The Minnesota Twins' Terry Ryan, who used to watch me as I groomed the fields in my 80s at the team's spring training complex in Fort Myers, Fla. Also, Bill Smith, Dave St. Peter and all the Twins' spring training staff, including groundskeeper P.J. Boutwell, Bill Hammond, John Yarbrough, Terry Slawson and Keith Blasingim. John, who has known me for 40 years, said, "George took groundskeeping to perfection." But he did have to correct me when I wanted some groundskeepers replaced when they didn't clean the dugouts properly. "They're county employees, George," he said. So I talked to them. Then there's one of my favorite fans, Syracuse Weaver. She'd bring me cookies every morning. Also can't forget Elliott Trumbull, who retired to Fort Myers after working for the Detroit Tigers.

Thanks to the Nashua Pride. Because of how much the New Hampshire owners respected my work, I had one of the best-paying consulting gigs I ever had in 2000. One Londonberry resident told Peter LeBlanc of The Derry News that Holman Stadium "looked better than Fenway Park."

To a terrific friend of mine, Rick Cerone, a former Yankees catcher who was owner of the Newark

Bears of the Independent Atlantic League. In 2001, I went to Newark, N.J., to help him break in a new groundskeeper. Rick knew what it took to have an excellent field from his playing days. He had a grounds crew and outstanding office people to work with.

The Denver Broncos and their dedicated groundskeeper, Steve Wightman. He also worked in San Diego.

The San Diego Padres and San Diego Chargers at Jack Murphy Stadium with Brian Bossard, Carlos Noriega, Bobby Slavy and Matt Balough.

Katie Deppen, who worked for Terry Porch with the Tennessee Titans, did fine work at the Super Bowl. Whether the job was clean or dirty, she got it done.

The Seattle Seahawks and Seattle Mariners at the Kingdome. It was a great pleasure working with all, especially Mark Duncan.

To Richard Okouda, manager for War Memorial Stadium in Maui, along with Myron Borge.

And to superintendent of grounds Mark Kubacki with St. Mary's College of Notre Dame.

To all the people associated with LSU football. In 2005, I prepared the team's playing field for home games due to the damage that Hurricane Katrina did to most of Louisiana. LSU had a terrific playing-field operation under the guidance of Todd Jeansonne and Jeff Kershaw, plus the great LSU grounds crew. After an LSU game on Saturday, we worked overnight on the field for an NFL game on

> Sunday. When I first got there, I asked Todd where we could get some airboats in order to dry the paint. He said, no problem, right across the street the college has six airboats. We met with the professor in charge of environmental studies. He said, "George, don't worry about handling them, I will have my students do all the work." Outstanding! Where else could you find such a generous man to help get some of the load off the grounds crew's shoulders? Here is what I call generosity, helping other people get their work done, plus helping to give the players a safe playing field. Yes, I'm extremely thankful to Todd and Jeff and all the LSU people who helped out. A sincere thank-you to everyone concerned!

So many people in the industry I want to thank:

> To Eddie Woerner and his family. I appreciate you for everything you have done for me and being so kind and considerate of me. You have truly shown me what friendship really means, and it also proves that the best things in life are those that are earned. A sincere thank-you for all you have done for me sodding fields. You never gave up and came up with new equipment to make our jobs easier. Yes, it has been some 30 years that we worked together on the mainland and with your Hawaii Turf Farm, helping us sod fields. I assure you that I value your friendship and on the top of my list is your late daughter, Brenda, who we lost at an early age. I enjoyed working with her, especially the outstanding job she did when we sodded the Superdome with sod 40 feet long by 7 feet wide. What the world needs today is more people like Brenda. Again, many thanks to you and Brenda. I'm wishing that you be repaid a thousand fold for all that you have done for me.

A sincere thank-you to Eddie Mangan. Really enjoyed working with you in those early years.

A special thank you and then some to Greg Harmour, World Class Athletic Surfaces for your friendship over many Super Bowls.

Thank you to moments of kindness so many people have showed me:

The past few years when I manicured the George P. Toma Wiffle Ball Field at the Hollow, Rebekah and Mark Stivers and Joe Ungashick's wife. Amy Cornwell always would bring me cold drinks. Rebekah and Mark also gave Donna a bag full of peaches from their trees. I didn't know Missouri could grow peaches!

Can't forget the Webbs, who we got to know when the Royals moved to Boardwalk and Baseball in Haines City, Fla. The Webbs sold citrus, candy and goat's milk fudge. They were such good people. When Hall of Famer Buck O'Neil came for spring training, they'd invite me and Buck over to their house for dinner. I also lived on the tomatoes and used to take strawberries home.

Thanks to Steve Hall, for his irrigation work in Haines City and also for giving Craig Handel my phone number. We have collaborated on this book.

To Clarence Grentencourd and family for that wonderful carrot cake and the Royals fans in the right field bullpen for all their goodies.

To longtime NFL assistant coach Tom Pratt and his wife, Hope Star Pratt, who have been in touch for the last 45 years.

To Bill McNutt, for sending me a fruitcake for the 57th straight year. One of the best deals I ever received.

Lisa O'Dell, a sincere thank you for your dedication in helping the wiffle ball players with their needs from pre-schoolers to senior citizens.

Thank you to those who wrote me letters and offered words of encouragement.

Former Kansas State football coach Bill Snyder, who led the greatest college football turnaround in history, left me this message: Hello, George, this is Bill Snyder just calling to see how you are doing, as well as to tell you how proud I have been to enjoy your work over the years. Best wishes to you and Donna as well. I hope this message finds you well, take care.

Special thanks to those who helped me personally:

Doctors Arthur McGhie, Ryan Lustig and Rebecca Doane.

Attorney Mike Atkins as well as John Parolin and family.

Then there's 'Dan the Man' LeBlanc, my assistant who I worked with on so many Super Bowls. He was a helluva groundskeeper.

Thanks to Nancy Finley and her father Carl. You know how I felt about your uncle, Charles O. Finley.

George C. Brown, the mayor of Wilkes-Barre, Pa.

A tip of the cap to Show Ikeda, who manicures soccer fields in Japan. He'd come to Super Bowls with three members of his crew. All he asked of the NFL was to put him up. Later, the NFL took him to China.

To the fans who came to games. When people came to spring training in Florida for the Royals and Twins and they had little kids, I'd let them come on the field and run around the bases or take pictures by home plate. I also had a pocket full of bubble gym, and on my way to the Royals' bullpen, I'd give the kids some gum or a ball if it was on the field. Just don't tell the dentists!

To Tony Dungy and Mike Tirico with NBC, Steve Mariucci with NFL Network, Howie Long with Fox and the rest of the sportscasters. A sincere thank-you for looking me up every Super Bowl game. Would you believe Tony Dungy came to the shop under the stands to find me at Super Bowl XLI when his Indianapolis Colts beat the Chicago Bears? The man never forgot the common touch.

Thanks to Dr. James R. Watson, Jim Steeg and the students at Lincoln High. You were the ones who made me.

A serious thank you and then some to Mike McDermott and Jerry Moore of the famous "Grass Pad" for all their help over the last 50 years.

Finally, I'd like to thank the groundskeepers from preschool to the pro level. The New York Giants' crew in Super Bowl XLVIII, thank you. In my book, they would get the game ball.

A special thank-you to our all-black grounds crew at Municipal Stadium for the Kansas City Athletics, Kansas City Chiefs, Kansas City Royals and Kansas City Spurs. Gino Armstrong, he was the leader. They gave Kansas City the best football, baseball and soccer fields, and we only spent $1,000 a year on materials. We got so fast at switching the field from baseball to football, we could do the operation in one day. Also, thanks to Steve Franzen, Raymond Hayward and Smokey Olson for helping out.

I made a lot of friendships in the baseball world. Mark Razum with the Colorado Rockies, Clay Wood with the Oakland Athletics, Grant Trenbeath with the Arizona Diamondbacks, Matt Balough with the San Diego Padres, Barney Lopas with the Anaheim Angels, Chad Mulholland with the Miami Marlins, Larry DiVito with the Minnesota Twins, Carrie Thomas and Heather Nabozny with the Detroit Tigers, Paul Zwaska with the Baltimore Orioles, Jim Anglea with the Texas Rangers, P.J. Boutwell with the Minnesota Twins in Fort Myers, Dave Mellor and Joe Mooney with the Boston Red Sox and, last but not least, Trevor Vance with the Kansas City Royals. Other men in heaven I want to thank: Emil Bossard with the Cleveland Indians, Harry Gill with the Milwaukee Brewers, Pat Santarone with the Baltimore Orioles and Dick Ericson with the Minnesota Twins.

I watched a lot of baseball and football during their 2023 seasons. So many outstanding grass fields. Travis Hogan and Kansas City. Tony Leonard and Philadelphia. The Miami Dolphins and the script writing in the end zone. The Baltimore Ravens field looked good all year. Jacksonville and Mark Clay and Nick Fedewa, good job. The Chicago Bears had Bermuda, and the field looked good, even in cold weather. Tampa Bay, just like the olden days when they had Wayne Ward. And Buffalo for the playoff game against the Pittsburgh Steelers. All those fans and groundskeepers getting the snow out of the stands and off the field. They did a helluva job. I bet that made Buffalo fan Mike Albino happy. Fans love to see the beauty of the fields on TV and when they attend the games. I talked to a few of the groundskeepers over the phone, but I'd just like to thank all of them in this book. Professional groundskeeping is in great hands. I'm so proud of a legacy that I helped create that just keeps getting better and better.

If I forgot anybody, please forgive me. I've been racking my brain so I don't leave anybody out. I'm 95, and my memory isn't as good as it used to be.

Just know, whether I mentioned you in print or not, you're in my thoughts and you're in my prayers.

God bless you all,

– George

Final Thoughts

In Malcolm Gladwell's terrific book *Outliers: The Story of Success*, he writes about the 10,000-hour rule.

Based on his research, he believes that becoming an expert in any skill is correctly practicing one's craft for at least 10,000 hours.

Where does that put groundskeeper George Toma? What would Mr. Gladwell think of the venerable groundskeeper who has worked at his craft for eight decades?

During my many chats with George, I started thinking about how many hours he worked from age 13 to 95. Based on what he and wife Donna told me, I started putting some numbers together.

Average hours worked per week: 70

Average weeks worked per year: 50

Years worked at that pace: 60

Approximate tally: 210,000 hours

When George wasn't groundskeeping, he mowed his neighbors' lawns. With a push mower.

For the other 20 years, which included groundskeeping while in high school and serving in the U.S. military during the Korean War, we're estimating he spent about 40 hours a week for 48 weeks.

That would be an additional 38,400 hours.

That would put the tally at roughly 250,000 hours.

Do you know anyone who has made that level of commitment to a vocation?

Even when George "retired," he figured he spent about 150 days away from home in his first six years as a consultant.

From the early days in Kansas City (above) until the later years working spring training games (below), George Toma maintained a relentless drive and passion that will be admired as much as his skill in manicuring sports fields.

This 5-foot-5 bundle of energy had an intense focus on his job. While working for the NFL in Germany on Nov. 9, 1989, he didn't realize until the next day that the Berlin Wall fell. This still amazes me, as his hotel was just a few blocks away from such a historic moment.

That's why in my 40-plus years of writing, I've never met anyone like him. Probably never will.

He turned watching grass grow into a main storyline in many Super Bowls.

What's admirable about George Toma is that he never became a groundskeeper to make a fortune. His overriding goal, his mantra, since he was a teen was to toil over a playing surface that players know would protect them.

"The best insurance for a ball player is a safe playing field," he has said time and again.

That's why George Toma wanted to write this book.

He takes such pride in safe fields and protecting players that it's incomprehensible to him that others wouldn't have the same ethics, the same commitment.

George Toma could have taken a different path. He could have become wealthy.

Kansas City Royals legend George Brett wanted to start a landscaping business with him.

The man who never went past high school spoke at various colleges on the subject of turf management. He did some commercials and endorsed some products, so imagine if he connected with a marketing firm.

His name was so powerful that companies donated, yes donated, equipment, fertilizer, and soil to the Kansas City Royals, the Super Bowl and the George P. Toma Wiffle Ball Field at the Hollow. That wiffle ball field has helped raise thousands of dollars for veterans and first responders suffering from post-traumatic stress disorder.

People he worked with in the industry even used his ideas to create side incomes. George never asked for a penny.

But he did all right. Executives from around the world marveled that George adapted to any situation that confronted him. As the boxer Mike Tyson once said, "Everyone has a plan until they get punched in the mouth."

Like a great chef guided by his taste buds and instinct, George addressed a field based on grass, soil, nutrients, equipment and weather. He then used various concoctions and mixes as well as techniques to make a field as level as a pool table. Trial and error he called it. This reminds me of a comment made by another creative mind, Thomas Edison: "I have not failed. I've just found 10,000 ways that won't work."

George welcomed challenges because when he fixed them, he became valuable.

Numerous city and team officials around the country offered him better deals to leave. He wanted to stay in Kansas City. He took the sport's toughest professional baseball job that offered the worst pay and earned the highest respect from titans such as soccer star Pele and NFL Commissioner Pete Rozelle.

That's how he worked the first 57 Super Bowls.

With a flair for promotion that Don King would be proud of, George put his profession in such a positive light that groundskeeping went from a disregarded job near the bottom of the totem pole to a highly respected position that earns media attention and allows top people in the field to command six-figure salaries.

What's one of sports' great debates?

Grass or artificial turf.

George did hundreds of interviews and had thousands of stories written on him. I know. He and his family shared the Toma Library with me. Boxes of clips from a variety of newspapers and magazines. Letters from NFL commissioners and people all around the country. Proclamations from all over the country. He wasn't just on the cover of the sports page but on the cover of the front page of the paper.

While he spoke to the media constantly, George quickly praised others, whether it was his grounds crew in Kansas

City, the Super Bowl or in Israel; NFL and Major League Baseball groundskeepers; former NFL executive Jim Steeg; Mayor Dianne Feinstein; or NFL commissioners Pete Rozelle, Paul Tagliabue and even Roger Goodell at times.

However, George never minced words. He wasn't afraid to speak his mind to those he felt deserved to be criticized. People such as Goodell.

My goal is that George's words unite the NFL power brokers – Goodell, owners, coaches and players – to make the fields as safe as possible, whether they have grass or artificial turf.

That's all the legacy this 95-year-old man needs.

– Craig Handel

Toma Timeline

1942: George Toma officially began his career as a groundskeeper at Artillery Park for the Wilkes-Barre Barons of the Class A Eastern League.

1946: Owner Bill Veeck promoted Toma to head groundskeeper.

1950 to 1953: Toma served in the Korean War with the United States Army.

1953: Toma joined the Detroit Tigers organization.

1955: Toma joined Triple-A Buffalo.

1956: Toma joined Triple-A Charleston.

November 1957: Offered jobs by both Kansas City and Denver, which was the New York Yankees' Triple-A affiliate, Toma chose Kansas City.

1957 to 1967: Toma was head groundskeeper for the Kansas City Athletics.

1960: Toma painted the field with the team's logo in the on-deck circle, an innovation at the time.

1963 to 1990: Toma was head groundskeeper for the Kansas City Chiefs. Paid by the Athletics and Kansas City Royals, Toma was loaned to the Chiefs.

1963: Using gold and red paint, Toma spelled out the word CHIEFS in the end zone before a game.

1966: Pete Rozelle said in a press conference that he never saw a better football field on a baseball field than at Municipal Stadium. He also wanted to have the same lettering the Chiefs used for the AFL-NFL championship game.

1966: Dallas Cowboys asked Toma to manicure the field for their Thanksgiving game vs. the Cleveland Browns. It was the Cowboys' first nationally televised game in color.

1966: NFL Commissioner Pete Rozelle asked Toma to be field supervisor for the first Super Bowl.

1967 to 2023: Toma worked every Super Bowl as either field supervisor or consultant. He is one of a handful of people who attended the first 57 Super Bowls.

1969 to 1995: Toma was head groundskeeper for Kansas City Royals.

1972: Both the Kansas City Royals and Kansas City Chiefs had new stadiums built in the Truman Sports Complex. Toma oversaw both fields.

1980 to 2016: NFL assigned Toma to manicure the field for each Pro Bowl at Aloha Stadium in Honolulu, Hawaii. The game was played there every year except for 2010 and 2015.

1980: Toma tried a blend of three turf-type rye grasses in Super Bowl XIV. From 1986 to 1987, the blend called Ph.D. was used in the Super Bowl, Fiesta Bowl, Rose Bowl and Orange Bowl.

1982: Toma was praised for his efforts in giving the San Francisco 49ers and Dallas Cowboys a field with solid footing for the 1981 season's NFC championship game. So impressed were Mayor Dianne Feinstein and San Francisco officials that they offered Toma a job. He declined.

1984: Toma restored the field for the Olympics in Los Angeles.

1993: Toma and his staff showed FIFA officials samples of grass grown on artificial turf, which played a big role in the organization designating the United States as the host country for the World Cup.

1995: The Royals returned to playing on a grass field.

1995: Toma was inducted into the International Hall of Fame of Science (pre-germination of grass-seed system).

1996: Toma restored the field for the Olympics in Atlanta.

1996: Toma was inducted into the Kansas City Walk of Stars.

1997: Toma spent three weeks in Israel rehabbing a combination softball-baseball field as well as a baseball field in Kibbutz Gezer for the Maccabiah Games.

1999: The New Orleans Saints and Green Bay Packers played an exhibition game in the Superdome on a grass field that Toma oversaw.

2001: Toma was inducted into the NFL Hall of Fame as a recipient of the Ralph Hay Pioneer Award.

I was fortunate enough to be among a small group of people that attended the first 57 Super Bowls. Above is a display of Super Bowl tickets from the first 41 NFL championship games.

2002: Lee County, Florida, officials hired Toma to rehab the Minnesota Twins' spring training fields.

2012: Toma was inducted into the Major League Baseball Groundskeepers Hall of Fame.

2012: Toma was inducted into the Kansas City Royals Hall of Fame.

2016: Toma was inducted into the Missouri Sports Hall of Fame.

2019: Jackson County, Mo., designated April 19 as George Toma Day.

2022: Toma was inducted into the Luzerne County Sports Hall of Fame in Pennsylvania.

2022: Toma was inducted into the Kansas Sports Hall of Fame.

2023: Toma was inducted into the North American Slovak Hall of Fame.

Chatting with good friend and former Kansas State football coach Bill Snyder.

In uniform on picture day before serving my country in the Korean War.

Bill Paprocki of the NFL Players Association had a George Toma bobblehead made. It was quite an honor and as far as I know the first bobblehead of a groundskeeper.

Above, I was featured on a billboard promoting Pennington Seed. Below, I joined Jim Ryun and good friend Buck O'Neil in the Kansas City Walk of Stars in 1996.

Taking a break with Andy Levy while we readied a field for play.

With P.J. Boutwell, left, and Keith Blasingim at Twins spring training in Fort Myers, Fla.

With former major leaguer Rex Hudler, accompanied by his son Cade, daughter Alyssa and wife Jennifer at the George P. Toma Wiffle Ball Field.

Posing with former Denver Broncos quarterback John Elway.

Sharing a few laughs with my good friend and Kansas City Royals legend George Brett.

Posing with Chiefs head groundskeeper Travis Hogan prior to kickoff at the Super Bowl.

Stealing a few batting practice swings in Kansas City.

Being honored by the Royals in a ceremony before the first pitch at Kauffman Stadium. | *Photo courtesy of the Kansas City Royals.*

Showing Mickey Mouse the proper technique for painting the field for Super Bowl Sunday.

About The Authors

George Toma

George Toma first worked as an assistant groundskeeper for the Class A Wilkes-Barre Barons in 1942, which led to an 80-year-plus career in maintaining and supervising some of the most iconic athletic fields in North American sports.

After working at various minor-league ballparks, Toma got his first taste of big-league groundskeeping in 1957 when he took a job with the Kansas City Athletics. He later became the Kansas City Chiefs' head groundskeeper from 1963 to 1990 and the Kansas City Royals' head groundskeeper from 1969 to 1995.

Toma worked the first 57 Super Bowls, either as head field supervisor or consultant. He also did groundskeeping work for NFL games played in Barcelona, London, Tokyo, Berlin and Mexico City.

His highly respected work led to other significant assignments, which included supervising the grounds crews during the 1984 and 1996 Olympic Games in Los Angeles and Atlanta and working at the 1994 World Cup.

Toma has been inducted into eight Halls of Fame.

Toma officially retired from full-time work in 1999 but then worked as a consultant for sports facilities and groundskeepers around the United States. Among the teams he worked with were the Minnesota Twins, who also employed his son Chip.

Toma, who turned 95 in 2024, lives in Westwood, Kan., with his wife, Donna.

Besides Chip, who's now retired, Toma has two other sons who carry on the family tradition of overachieving at work. Rick works for Servbank as the chief operating officer, and Ryan is a first officer for Delta Airlines.

There are seven grandchildren – Brandy, Amanda, Alysse, Katie, Elizabeth, Addison and Joey – as well as eight great-grandchildren – Olivia, Sophia, Grace, Bella, Cali, Kenny, Stetson and Georgia.

Just down the street from where the Tomas live is the George P. Toma Wiffle Ball Field at the Hollow, where wiffle ball games are played all summer long.

The field has helped raise more than $1.5 million to help veterans and first responders suffering from post-traumatic stress disorder.

After putting countless hours into restoring the field in 2019 and 2020, Toma still comes around to ensure the grass is lush and green. In other words, it's pristine.

Craig Handel

Craig Handel has written for newspapers in Wisconsin, Arizona, California, Massachusetts and Florida since he started writing in junior high.

Inspired by his librarian and journalism teacher, he had his first published story in eighth grade. He sold newspaper subscriptions to earn enough money to buy a cassette recorder.

In college, he earned degrees in broadcast and print journalism at Wisconsin-Eau Claire.

Craig also has collaborated on six other books focused on diverse topics ranging from tales from an Irish storyteller, a way to optimize mental performance in sports and business, a New Jersey entrepreneur who became a self-made millionaire, a female entrepreneur who mastered in buying real estate in Southwest Florida and building and developing nonprofits.

He considers being a consultant on the documentary Curveballs ... Secrets to the Game of Life with John Biffar and David Van Sleet to be one of the most inspiring and rewarding projects in his life. He feels the men featured on this amputee baseball team offer an amazing perspective on overcoming adversity and living a life of purpose and meaning.

As a writer, Craig feels there's a strong correlation between a great story and great quotes while there's also a correlation between great quotes and the questions that are asked. This formula is one of the main ingredients in this book on George Toma as well as other books he's written.

An avid gardener and swimmer, Craig lives with wife Isabel and their puppy Ollie in St. Petersburg, Florida.

Thank You

Thank you so much for reading this book. It has been a pleasure to share my experiences with you. If you enjoyed this book, please consider leaving a book review on the website where you bought the book.

Made in the USA
Monee, IL
19 November 2024

70448317R00164